THE WEEKDAY CHURCH SCHOOL

How to Organize and Conduct a Program of
Weekday Religious Education
on Released Time

ERWIN L. SHAVER

Published for the
Co-operative Publication Association

THE PILGRIM PRESS · BOSTON

Contents

THE CO-OPERATIVE SERIES
LEADERSHIP TRAINING TEXTS

Many thousands of lay workers in Protestant churches attend interdenominational leadership education schools each year. It is essential that the courses offered and the text materials used be acceptable to the many varieties of Protestant groups found in our American communities.

The Co-operative Series of leadership education textbooks are produced to meet that need. They are planned by the Division of Christian Education of the National Council of the Churches of Christ in the U. S. A., representing thirty-nine Protestant denominations. The Co-operative Publication Association, an interdenominational group of denominational editors and publishers, selects the writers and provides editorial supervision to insure sound educational values, practical usefulness and interdenominational approval and acceptance.

The Author's Foreword

IN 1921, at the request of the Religious Education Association, the author was granted a leave of absence from his college teaching to survey the extent and character of the new schools of religion for children excused from the public school. Ever since, he has watched the progress of this movement with interest and expectation, especially the last dozen years during which he has served as Executive Director of Weekday Religious Education for the Division of Christian Education of the National Council of Churches and its predecessor organization, the International Council of Religious Education. It was logical, therefore, that he should accept the invitation of the Co-operative Publication Association to prepare this text for use in leadership education schools and for the reading and study of all persons who may be interested.

The central purpose of the book is to give practical help both to those who are considering the establishment of a weekday church school program and to those who, having established such a program, feel the need for improving and strengthening it. The writer proceeds on the assumption that this type of religious education agency is here to stay, and discusses only incidentally the controversial questions which have, until recently, been raised with regard to it.

If the careful student should note that certain statements are repeated in various portions of the treatment, let it be said that this has been deliberate, both because of the interrelatedness of various aspects of the subject and the need for re-emphasis of key ideas. If the reader does not catch the restatement, it is an indication that the repetition has been necessary; if he does, it will reinforce the importance of it in his mind.

As will be noted from the contents, the author is indebted to a number of individuals and groups for references to and quotations from their statements. For their contributions he is grateful and makes this public acknowledgment of them.

Our book has no formal dedication. If there were to be one, it would have to include many, many friends of the weekday religious education movement who have in person, by correspondence, and in their indefatigable labors for the cause, strengthened the arm and warmed the heart of the writer. The members of the National Council of Churches' Committee on Weekday Religious Education and its associated Weekday Religious Education Section may be considered as representative of the larger circle. These two groups have shared most generously in carrying the responsibilities for the weekday program. To all these, professionals and laymen together, this volume of guidance is dedicated.

E. L. S.

Winnipesaukee, New Hampshire.

Chapter I

Enter: The Weekday Church School

A NEW CHARACTER has come upon the stage to play a prominent role in the unfolding drama of Christian education — the weekday church school. Dr. Percy R. Hayward has given us a revealing vignette of this new school in these dynamic sentences:

" The Weekday Church School was nurtured in the heart of a superintendent of schools who sensed the kinship of religion and education.

" From that beginning almost half a century ago, it has spread across the land and now is found in distant country communities, in a host of small towns, and amid the rush of great cities.

" It lifts religion out of its restricted home in one day of the week and in one place and makes it at home in every day and in any place.

" Under its touch religion becomes the companion of science, the interpreter of history, the crown of all the learning of the schools.

" It brings the redeeming touch of spiritual ideals to a multitude whom the churches do not reach. It enriches and reinforces the teaching of the church to a host now within her folds.

" The Weekday Church School holds in its hands the possibility of a new citizenship.

" It points the way by which the holy purpose of the Fathers of the Nation, to lay its foundation in religion, can be achieved.

" It carries the support of the makers of the public schools.

" It has called upon ministers and laymen, teachers and home makers, parents and professors for its support, and they have not failed.

" Grasp it boldly, all of you who carry the destiny of a nation on your hearts, use it with sacrifice and devotion, and it will strengthen and consummate all other forces that seek to follow the ancient Word, 'Righteousness exalteth a nation.' " [1]

It is the purpose of this volume to describe this new agency of Christian education in some detail: its origin and history; its organization and administration; its teaching program and materials; its leadership; its relationships to the several other educational agencies of the church and community; the ways of securing its support by the community; and the standards set for its success as a worthy unit in the churches' total program of Christian education.

THE NEW SCHOOL DEFINED

Briefly, " a weekday church school is a school set up by the churches in co-operation or individually, in which the attending pupils are excused from the public school at the written request of parents, to go to a church or other building to receive religious education." [2]

This new school for the religious education of children

---

[1] *Remember the Weekday to Teach Religion Thereon* (National Council of Churches), p. 2.

[2] *Ibid.*, p. 5.

and youth has a variety of patterns. To attempt a description of many of them would be difficult and impracticable within the limited scope of our text. Three major types, however, are to be found. The first is a school set up and conducted by one local church with no relationship to similar schools which may be operated by other churches in the community. This is known as the parish or denominational weekday church school, and is preferred by some religious groups. The second type is similar to the first in that each church maintains its own school. The several churches, however, co-operate in such matters as choosing an advisory committee or board, and in planning jointly for pupil excusal and class schedules, for dealing with the public school and other agencies, for common publicity and promotion, and occasionally for a common curriculum.

The third type is known as the co-operating or community weekday church school. In this type the Protestant and other religious groups which may care to do so, organize a single weekday church school system, operating its several schools or centers without regard to denominational lines, selecting teachers in like manner, choosing a curriculum to be used throughout the system, and housing the classes in the church or other building which is found most suitable. The great majority of communities in which weekday religious education is conducted make use of this co-operative type of program. The particular values of these several types will be treated later. [3]

As indicated in our brief definition, weekday church schools are conducted on school time on the same basis that religion is taught within school time in a private or parochial school. However, for varied reasons, a number of individual

[3] See page 37.

church and community schools operate outside of school hours. Much of what we shall say with regard to programs on released time will apply to these others also.

RELIGION IN THE CHILD'S WEEKDAY LIFE

Why are religion and religious education needed in the weekday life of our children today? Here are some reasons:

1. In the face of the complex social problems which characterize today's society and the consequent increasingly difficult task of Christian character development, much more religious training is needed than we are accustomed to provide through the limited program of the Sunday church school, no matter how good this may be.

2. Vast changes in the religious groupings now to be found in America have made it less and less easy to deal with religion in our public schools.

3. The greater emphasis upon the social and physical sciences in public education has tended — except where these scientific facts are given a religious interpretation — toward an increasingly secular and humanistic view of life.

4. Religion taught apart from the child's everyday educational program, on Sunday alone or on marginal time, seems in the child's mind to be of less significance than the other studies he pursues in his general education program.

5. To meet and overcome the more numerous and more highly organized temptations to delinquency, more and better teaching of religion is needed than in previous generations.

GOALS OF THE WEEKDAY CHURCH SCHOOL

The objectives of Christian education on the weekday are those of Christian education generally. Statements of these goals have been made from time to time by denominational and interdenominational agencies. Two of the best known statements are the *Objectives of Christian Education* and the *Goals for the Christian Education of Children*, both adopted by the Division of Christian Education of the National Council of Churches. We quote the first and briefer of these two statements:

I. Christian education seeks to foster in growing persons a consciousness of God as a reality in human experience, and a sense of personal relationship to him.

II. Christian education seeks to develop in growing persons such an understanding and appreciation of the personality, life and teachings of Jesus as will lead to experience of him as Savior and Lord, loyalty to him and his cause, and will manifest itself in daily life and conduct.

III. Christian education seeks to foster in growing persons a progressive and continuous development of Christlike character.

IV. Christian education seeks to develop in growing persons the ability and disposition to participate in and contribute constructively to the building of a social order throughout the world, embodying the ideal of the fatherhood of God and the brotherhood of man.

V. Christian education seeks to develop in growing persons the ability and disposition to participate in the organized society of Christians — the Church.

VI. Christian education seeks to develop in growing persons an appreciation of the meaning and importance of the Christian family, and the ability and disposition to participate in and contribute constructively to the life of this primary social group.

VII. Christian education seeks to lead growing persons into a Christian interpretation of life and the universe; the ability to see in it God's purpose and plan; a life philosophy built upon this interpretation.

VIII. Christian education seeks to effect in growing persons the assimilation of the best religious experience of the race, pre-eminently that recorded in the Bible, as effective guidance to present experience.[4]

What specific contributions to the achievement of these inclusive Christian education goals does the weekday church school make? These contributions are to be thought of, not so much as additions to the goals, as opportunities for emphases which its unique characteristics make possible. For example:

1. The weekday church school, in furnishing more time for Christian education, allows for a stronger teaching impact and a greater likelihood of progress toward these goals. Among others a " consciousness of God " and an " appreciation of Jesus," by this additional time provision, are deepened and lead to a clearer understanding and a closer personal relationship.

2. The opportunity for repetition which weekday church school sessions give fulfills an important educational principle. Christian character growth requires repeated practice under guidance.

3. The holding of the classes on the weekday not only reinforces the Sunday teaching, but because of the time factor strengthens the importance of religion in " daily life and conduct."

4. The relationship of the weekday church school to the public school allows for a significant correlation of the study of religion with public school studies. The closer this correlation, the greater the development of a consistent and integrated " Christian interpretation of life and the universe."

[4] *Christian Education Today* (National Council of Churches).

5. The *school* atmosphere characteristic of most weekday religious education is a helpful complement to the equally valuable *church* atmosphere provided by other agencies of Christian education. This tends to strengthen the pupils' respect for the study of religion.

6. The nature of the weekday church school in its organization and pattern makes it possible to reach a high proportion of children unrelated to the church and lead them to " participate in the organized society of Christians — the Church."

In comparing the goals of Christian education with those of general education, distinguishing relationships such as these may be noted:

1. The weekday church school allows for the inclusion of the *positive* teaching of religion and the Bible in the child's everyday education, which cannot be done in the public school.

2. Similarly Christian teaching which emphasizes personal commitment and church membership, not possible in public education, can be carried on with freedom.

3. The weekday church school, to fulfill its objectives completely, can and should supplement the social studies taught in the public school by giving them a Christian interpretation and motivation.

4. Likewise, the weekday church school can and should complement the physical science studies of the public school by insisting that underlying scientific laws and facts are the purposes of a wise and beneficent God.

5. The literature of the Bible and other religious literature taught in the weekday church school are a needed supplement to and natural enrichment of the literature studies program of the public school.

6. The weekday church school teaching program — affirming faith in the fatherhood of God as well as in the brotherhood of man — gives both motivation and content for the teaching of spiritual values in the public school, without which these values may not be distinguished from community ethics.

RELIGION IN EARLY AMERICAN EDUCATION

A brief statement should be made with regard to the place of religion in the educational systems of the colonies and throughout the first half century of the new United States. Our schools, locally organized and functioning, were almost all church established and controlled. The Bible and religious exercises were central in the curriculum. Their ultimate purpose was primarily religious, even though " the three R's " furnished the content. In those areas of America where there was one established church, as in New England and Virginia, these schools may be said to have been community in nature; in other areas, where a variety of sects had equal privileges, as in Pennsylvania, the schools were largely parochial in character.

THE EDUCATIONAL REVOLUTION

This condition, with some changes and variations, continued until the selection of Horace Mann as secretary of the Massachusetts State Board of Education in 1837. In this commonwealth, during the four preceding decades, there had been a radical change in the number and character of the religious groups and in addition a cataclysmic division between the Trinitarian and Unitarian branches of established Congregationalism. When Mann found that there was a vast amount of " doctrinal religion," that is, sectarian religious instruction in the schools, he began his two-front campaign. He set out to rid the schools of sectarian control and instruction. At the same time he hoped to discover what he was accustomed to call " the religion of heaven," which should be taught in the schools. Said he, " I am in favor of religious instruction in our schools, to the extremest verge to which it can be carried without invading those rights of conscience which are established by the laws of God, and guaranteed to us by the Constitution of the State." Again he said, " Had the Board required me to exclude the Bible or religious instruction from the schools, I certainly should have given them the earliest opportunity to appoint my successor."

Horace Mann has rightly been called " the father of the American public school system." His successful battle to rid the public schools of sectarian domination and teaching will ever be a milestone in the history of American education. But, in recognizing his unsurpassed contribution to our secular educational system, we must not forget his equally determined purpose to keep religion in that system. His failure to find " the religion of heaven " which would fulfill that objective was a great disappointment to him in his later years. As a recent writer has put it, " Reluctantly, and with a pessimistic judgment on education without religious teaching at the heart of it, he abandoned his hopes."[5]

A REAWAKENED CONCERN

The torch which Horace Mann carried in behalf of religious instruction in the public schools may be said to have almost gone out in the century which has elapsed since his day. Not quite, however, for to some degree his purpose has been kept alive by various persons and movements. Within

[5] Bayne, Stephen F., Jr., *The Optional God* (New York: Oxford University Press).

the past decades there has developed a revival of concern for the inclusion of religion in the child's general education. Various plans and proposals have been put forth and have received varying amounts of experimentation and testing.

The weekday church school, providing for the positive teaching of religion under church auspices and within the hours set apart by law and custom for formal education, is one of these plans. Other contributions toward a solution of the problem are the proposals to emphasize the factual study of religion (or teaching *about* religion) in the public school and to make generous use of religious resources in their natural relationship to the various areas of study comprising the public school curriculum. These latter proposals are the responsibility of the public school and are not to be considered alternatives to nor substitutes for such a church-sponsored program as the weekday church school on released time, with which this text is concerned.

BASIC CHARACTERISTICS

The relationships of the weekday church school to the public school suggest certain basic characteristics of the new agency of Christian education which mark it as different from other church educational programs. One of these is the expectation that weekday church school teachers, supervisors, and directors should be professional in the sense that they should have training equal to that of the public school leaders and that they should give all or a portion of their time and interest to this calling. This expectation is no disparagement of the self-sacrificing volunteer leadership given to other programs of the church.[6] It grows out of

[6] The author in his *Shall Laymen Teach Religion?* makes a strong plea for the use of lay workers under guidance in the Sunday church school and certain other educational activities of the church.

a deep-seated conviction that the message of the Gospel deserves a quality of teaching commensurate with its high character as well as a vital Christian experience for the teacher.

Obviously, the use of professional leadership will greatly increase the outlay for Christian education. Friends of the weekday church school hold that its expenditure for the teaching of religion should be at least equivalent to that paid for the teaching of public school subjects. In this respect the weekday church school movement has set a new and higher goal for the financial support of Christian education.

There are a number of other characteristics basic to this type of church school, but we conclude our comments in this area with one more — the conviction that the most effective weekday church schools are those in which the several Protestant groups pool their resources in a common teaching program rather than conducting separate programs of a denominational character in each individual church. This community approach has been one of the pioneer demonstrations of ecumenicity and its success has been most marked.

A PRODUCT OF THE RELIGIOUS EDUCATION MOVEMENT

The entrance of the weekday church school upon the Christian education scene is one of the expressions of the religious education movement of the last fifty years. This movement has had as its objective more and better education in religion. Another expression was the founding of the Religious Education Association in 1903, which stated its three-fold purpose thus:

" (1) To inspire the religious forces of our country with the educational ideal, (2) to inspire the educational forces with the religious ideal, (3) to keep before the public the ideal of religious education and the sense of its need and value."

Still another expression of this movement was the merger of the International Sunday School Association and the Sunday School Council of Evangelical Denominations in 1922 to form the International Council of Religious Education.

In view of the advances made by our public schools this last half century, it is but natural that religious education leaders should have given their attention to the development of better teaching methods, better curriculum materials, better housing and equipment, and better financial undergirding for the teaching of religion. It is likewise understandable that a wider expansion of the religious education program should have come about, as evidenced by fifty years of successful experience with the vacation church school and the summer camp and conference, as well as by the four-decade growth of the weekday church school.

The impact of the social action movement upon religious education has greatly aided the trend to apply religion to weekday affairs. A more serious emphasis upon the teaching function of the church has brought together kindred minds and furthered the co-operative approach to various religious education projects, especially the programs of leadership education and the weekday teaching program.

Central also in the total movement has been the emphasis upon a professionally trained church leadership including directors of religious education, college pastors, and teachers and supervisors of weekday church schools.

Another factor stimulating the development of weekday

church schools has been the steadily growing conviction that the church should have a fair share of the educational time of boys and girls and correlatively the insistence that their education should not become a monopoly on the part of the state. One other characteristic of the weekday church school program is that it is free from fixed patterns and therefore unhampered by " we've always done it this way."

In these various ways weekday church schools have both shared in and contributed to the total religious education movement.

FAVORED BY PUBLIC EDUCATORS

For the most part public education leaders have been as staunch supporters of the weekday church school movement as church leaders have been. As our opening quotation reveals, " the weekday church school was nurtured in the heart of a superintendent of schools who sensed the kinship of religion and education." This pioneer public educator was William Wirt, superintendent of schools of Gary, Indiana. Since his day thousands of teachers, principals, and superintendents of public schools have endorsed and strongly supported weekday church school programs in their communities. Typical of their beliefs in this program is the statement of Principal Marvin J. Schmitt of the Lincoln Public School in Oak Park, Illinois, where a weekday church school system has been in operation since 1920: " There is no question in my mind, but that most children who have been and are enrolled in the weekday program of religious education *are* benefited. It *does* make a difference." [7]

A few years ago the National Education Association's

[7] " I Believe in Weekday Religious Education," *International Journal of Religious Education.*

Research Division published a report surveying the weekday church school, or " released time " programs held in connection with the American public schools. In this study it was noted that the attitude of the public school teaching staff to the program was exceedingly favorable. Five-sixths of the reports from the 708 school systems, in relation to which some kind of formal religious education program was in operation, contained answers indicating " the attitude of the majority of the school system's teaching staff." Of these five-sixths, " 82% indicated that the teaching staff is favorable toward the religious education program, and 18% unfavorable." [8]

This earnest and sympathetic support of weekday church schools on the part of public school workers has, in fact, sometimes been a source of embarrassment to church leaders. The latter, through indifference, slowness, and ignorance, have found themselves quite unprepared to launch a program when the initiative of excusing children for this purpose has been taken by school leaders. Since the highly favorable decision by the United States Supreme Court in 1952 there have been additional evidences of this readiness on the part of public school men to co-operate in the weekday church school program.

PARENTS WANT WEEKDAY CHURCH SCHOOLS

One indication among others that weekday church schools are welcomed by parents is found in the high percentage of children enrolled who have no other connection with a church or church school. There are various reasons why the parents of these un-churched, as well as of those of church-related children, are glad to take advantage of this

[8] *The Status of Religious Education in the Public Schools* (Washington, D. C.: National Education Association, 1949), p. 12.

new agency of religious education. For many, enrollment in the weekday school of religion is the first step toward attending Sunday church school and becoming a church member. In some communities as high as seventy per cent of the weekday school enrollment is un-churched. The average proportion throughout the years of the movement's development has been about twenty-five per cent.

Technically and practically the weekday church school is a parents' school. Basically the educational system of America is what the citizen parents want it to be. The freedom to choose the kind of education and the kind of school — public, private, or parochial — which their children shall attend is one of our cherished freedoms. Now that the parent's right to have his child excused from the public school for systematized religious education has been declared constitutional, it is hoped that parents will more and more take advantage of this privilege.

PUPILS LIKE THE WEEKDAY CHURCH SCHOOL

For the most part the pupils who attend the weekday church school have a real appreciation of its values. They have developed a higher regard for religion. They have found it helpful in daily life. They have acquired a greater factual knowledge of the Bible and other religious literature. They have come to know and love the teacher of religion and have caught something of her spiritual strength. They have developed a more mature and confident trust in God. These values have found expression in countless testimonies reported by many weekday systems. Here are a few samples:[9]

[9] From the *Council Reporter*, a publication of the Boston Council of Weekday Religious Education, Esther B. Stricker, Supervisor.

I cannot tell you how much I enjoy religious education and how much it has helped me to be a better person. I know it has cost you a lot of money and from the bottom of my heart I thank you.

— A sixth grade pupil

I have learned a lot from the references and Bible stories in Sunday school, sermons, or in confirmation, but never in such detail as here.

— A ninth grade pupil

This course of study has made me think twice about my religion. It has made me believe that my religion as a Protestant is true, and when people say it isn't true, then I will tell them why I believe in it.

— A ninth grade pupil

You will be interested to know that I have decided to go into full time religious service. I am now in college, but feel that I will have to change my course, since I just can't get away from the desire to prepare for church work.

— A former pupil

One of the high-light moments in the trial of the Champaign, Illinois, weekday religious education program came when James Terry McCollum was asked why he wanted to enroll in the classes in religion. Among several reasons he frankly gave were these:

I was interested in this class in religious education. I wanted to take it. . . . I do not like arithmetic and spelling very well. I like religious education a lot better. I recall that Miss Chapin brought in school a lot of different papers and things, and sometimes the kids passed one on my desk. I was also interested in the little ornaments she brought from China and different places. . . . I wanted to hear Miss Chapin's opinion. . . . One of the reasons I liked to take the religious education course was because

I was anxious to know the way they taught them. . . . I kind of want to know a little more about religion. I do not know much about it. . . . After I took the course when I was in fourth grade I wanted to learn still more. I enjoyed the work over there.[10]

The natural interest and curiosity of this boy, whose home pressure was against joining the classes in religion, was after all not unlike that of thousands of other children who enroll in weekday church schools with the encouragement of their parents.

IN THE AMERICAN TRADITION

The centrality of religion in American life — in government as well as in the lives of individual citizens — is traditional and deeply rooted. Our people, from the time of the Declaration of Independence until now, have affirmed their belief in God and his provident guidance. Our history as a nation; our national, state, and local laws; our practices in every branch of government — legislative, executive, and judicial — all give testimony to the value of religious faith and that faith which rests upon the existence and rule of a Supreme Judge of Nations.

What we ourselves hold as citizens we are in duty bound to teach to our children. To eliminate religion from our system of education would be utterly inconsistent with our system of government. Education, as one of the great national interests, must have a place for the teaching of religion. Throughout the years since Horace Mann we have sought an answer to this problem. We believe that in the weekday church school we have found an answer, not the only one, but nevertheless a practical and effective one.

[10]Abstract of Record in the case of Vashti McCollum vs. Board of Education of School District 71, in Circuit Court of Champaign County, pp. 228-230.

Chapter II

The New School Is Tested

THE WEEKDAY church school has had to meet severe tests to establish and maintain its standing in the religious education world. While some of these tests have been annoying and often difficult to understand, they have after all been good for the movement. There has been the test of time, a measure of effectiveness which every new development has had to meet. There has been and will continue to be the test of educational quality, for unless the new program can live up to the uniquely high level of religious education envisioned by its originators, it will go the way of other forgotten projects. There has been the test of legality, a trial indeed for the friends of the new program, but one which happily has been passed through victoriously. There has been the test of financial support, a doubly severe one: the higher level of expenditure required for this type of Christian education and the willingness to invest denominational funds in a co-operative enterprise. There has been the test of wholehearted acceptance by the churches on a national scale. One of the purposes of this volume is to assist the various Protestant groups, national and local, to see clearly the great possibilities in weekday religious education and to give it the moral, financial, and educational support without which it cannot succeed.

FOUR DECADES OF GROWTH

It is not our intent to give details with respect to the history of the weekday religious education movement, nor to endeavor to locate the very earliest school of this type, of which there were doubtless a number. Rather it is to present a brief panorama of the movement's progress during these more than forty years, which may be divided roughly into ten-year periods.

The first decade may be characterized as *a period of beginnings*. The experiment begun in Gary, with the co-operation of Superintendent Wirt and the Protestant ministers in the fall of 1914, represents the establishment of a pattern for elementary weekday religious education which has been followed extensively throughout the land. The movement for weekday religious education at the secondary school level, which for various reasons has had a less extensive growth, antedated the Gary system by two years. The " seminary " program, begun in Salt Lake City under the auspices of the Church of Jesus Christ of Latter Day Saints in 1912, has had a remarkable success. Other high school level programs have since been established on an inter-church basis in the Carolinas, the Virginias, and Texas, and to a lesser degree elsewhere. It is the elementary school program, however, which has given the weekday religious education movement its name and public acceptance.

The year 1922 represents the beginning of the second decade of development. Following a survey of the new movement, made in that year by the Religious Education Association, the growth of these schools was greatly accelerated. This period of rapid expansion saw programs established in two hundred communities in twenty-three states and enrolling some forty thousand pupils. It was but natural that such a rapid growth should result in some ill-advised as well as some soundly based programs. It was in this period that the use of public school classrooms and machinery became a more common although unwise practice, in spite of warnings from within and without the movement. During this period much publicity was given the new agency, some of it helpful, and some less so. A number of surveys and studies were made, including one by the United States Office of Education. The states began to pass enabling acts to confirm the legality of the practice of excusing pupils for this purpose. Several denominations were employing persons giving full time to the guidance of the new type program. The various schools of religious education were giving increased attention to preparing directors and teachers for this professionally led movement. Unfortunately, if this second decade of weekday church school expansion were to be evaluated, it would probably have to be said that it was *a period of "mushroom growth."*

By 1932 " the depression " was on in full force. This resulted in the breakdown of a number of weekday systems and the shifting from paid to volunteer leadership on the part of others. On the whole, however, it slowed up the movement only slightly, for the number of programs still continued to increase. Four hundred communities in thirty states were enrolling some two hundred and fifty thousand pupils in weekday schools of religion in the early part of this decade. At the end of the decade the Department of Weekday Religious Education of the International Council of Religious Education reported that the program was operating in eighteen hundred communities in forty-six states and that a million and a half pupils were attending week-day church schools. The movement had become *practically nation wide*.

The fourth decade in the history of the weekday church school movement began with *legal opposition* which proved to be extensive. In addition to several local legal battles, the famous Champaign case was initiated by Mrs. Vashti McCollum in 1945, and was carried successively to the Illinois Supreme Court and the United States Supreme Court. In 1948 two cases were started in New York City, the second of which was finally brought to the United States Supreme Court. We shall give more details of these cases later. Although the attention and efforts of the friends of the movement were necessarily directed to the legal situation, other developments within the movement were taking place. The International Council of Religious Education gave added help and guidance to the new movement, increasing the services of a director from half time to full time. The membership of the Council's Committee on Weekday Religious Education more than tripled during this time, and the membership of the Weekday Religious Education Section, a body of professional weekday leaders, reached a total of almost two hundred and fifty from a beginning thirty years previously of some twenty-five members.

SURVEYS AND STUDIES

Almost from the beginning the movement for week-day religious education has been the object of scrutiny and examination. It is fortunate that the Religious Education Association, as previously reported, undertook to appraise the plan only seven years after the Gary plan was launched. In preparation for a three days' discussion a questionnaire survey was made of some 324 centers, and personal visits to 42 of these were made by the writer of this volume. We quote excerpts from the report of the convention's Findings Committee:

> We recognize in this new movement what may prove to be a most effective agency . . . provided that, at its inception it has the guidance of a trained leadership moving toward carefully defined aims and taking advantage of the best that modern education has to offer.

> This movement at present represents a fine expression of religious devotion with a recognition that something is wrong, or at least inadequate in our present programs of education. . . .

> The weekday school is challenged by both the public school and the child to justify its claim for a share of their time and attention. . . . This is a legitimate challenge and one that the school of religion must frankly meet. Provided this challenge is met, however, the school of religion is entitled to the opportunity to make its vital contribution to the education of the child. . . .

> The work of religious instruction and training should be done by such institutions as the home, the church, and the private school, and not by the public school nor in official connection with the public school. . . .

> It is apparent that high standards of professional training for teachers are a requisite for the success of weekday programs of religious education. . . .

> The weekday religious school seems to give hope of realizing for the modern world a religious training more nearly adequate to meet present conditions. . . . If it follows the trend which seems to represent the conviction of this convention and is embodied in these findings, we

shall find in it a most significant agency of religious education.[1]

Had these recommendations been more widely circulated and had their warnings been heeded, we believe the weekday movement would have been freer from difficulties and less subject to criticism, particularly with respect to its legal status, but also because of its failure, in a number of communities, to maintain expected educational standards.

A large number of students have chosen to investigate this new church school program, particularly in recent years. But even in the early years there were careful researches conducted for which we are greatly indebted. P. Henry Lotz, then a student at Northwestern University, personally visited and studied 109 centers of weekday religious instruction and published his results in the volume, *Current Weekday Religious Education*, in 1925.[2] Another study, *Religious Education on Public School Time*, was made in 1926 by F. S. Gove, a student at the Harvard Divinity School.[3] Donald R. Gorham, in the Graduate School of Eastern Baptist Theological Seminary, did likewise and compiled his findings in 1934 under the title, *The Status of Protestant Weekday Church Schools in the United States*.[4]

An evaluational study reported by Edward R. Bartlett, also of the Northwestern University, was focussed on the question of the extent to which the pupils in weekday religious education classes profited from the experience. He found that there were appreciable results from the program conducted in the weekday church school system of Oak

[1] Cope, Henry F. (editor), *Weekday Religious Education* (Doran), pp. 170-172.
[2] Published by Abingdon Press, New York.
[3] Published by Harvard University, Cambridge.
[4] Published by the Eastern Baptist Theological Seminary, Philadelphia.

Park, Illinois, which he selected as his research laboratory. His study was published in *Religious Education*, January, 1934, under the title "Measurable Moral and Religious Outcomes of Weekday Religious Instruction."

There have been two published studies of the movement at the high school level. One of these was made by Kenneth L. Thompson in 1938. It was based upon an investigation of the secondary level programs and was published in a monograph entitled *Weekday Religious Education in the High Schools of the United States.*[5] More recently Lois V. McClure, a graduate student at Northwestern University, at the request of the International Council of Religious Education, made a thorough study of the secondary level programs throughout the country and published her results in *Religious Education* under the title "Weekday Religious Education at the High School Level."[6]

In 1932 and again in 1941 the United States Office of Education surveyed the growth of weekday religious education classes. Another extensive study, previously mentioned, was made by the National Education Association's Division of Research.[7] This was published in 1949 on the basis of the situation existing in 1948 following the Supreme Court's decision in the much-discussed McCollum Case. It furnished helpful information as to the spread of the weekday program, including both existing and discontinued systems.

COUNSELING BY THE COUNCILS

Throughout the development of the movement the Protestant national interdenominational agencies interested in

[5] Published by the Eastern Baptist Theological Seminary, Philadelphia.
[6] Reprints of this study are available from the National Council of Churches.
[7] *The Status of Religious Education in Public Schools* (Washington, D. C.: National Education Association).

religious education have been concerned with the progress and quality of the programs in operation and those projected. The Department of Weekday Religious Education of the National Council of Churches has given counsel as to standards, curriculum materials, leadership, legal, and other areas of need through office visits, correspondence, and field trips. It has issued reports upon the progress and problems of the weekday schools. It has prepared bulletins and published articles in various denominational and interdenominational magazines, particularly the *International Journal of Religious Education* and *Religious Education*. Twice the Department promulgated statements of policy with respect to the weekday church school program, once in 1941 and again in 1949 following the Champaign case decision.[8] Both of these statements of policy adopted by the former International Council of Religious Education were reaffirmed by the Division of Christian Education of the National Council of Churches. A central purpose of the Weekday Department's activities has been the setting and maintenance of high standards so that the movement may meet successfully the test of educational quality.

SETTLING THE LEGAL ISSUE

More than a quarter of a century ago, Edward Sargent, the director of weekday religious education of the Protestant Episcopal Church, prophesied that the weekday movement would pass through three stages: first, " rapid mushroom growth "; second, " legal fighting for existence "; and third, the need for " higher standards." Having indicated something of the rapid growth, we shall comment briefly on

[8] See page 137.

the happenings during the second stage, which we believe has now been passed successfully.

In 1926 suit was brought against the weekday church school program conducted in White Plains, New York, by Joseph Lewis, the president of the American Free Thinkers Society, on the grounds that it violated the principle of separation of church and state. The legal validity of the program was sustained unanimously by the highest court of the state. In 1940, to insure the free and effective working of the increasing number of weekday church school systems throughout the state of New York, an amendment to the state school code was passed allowing for the excusal of pupils for " religious observance and education."

For some twenty years the program developed free from legal opposition. Twelve states and two territories [9] passed laws to give legal confirmation to the growing practice. But again the program was contested, this time with great vigor and much national publicity. In June, 1945, Mrs. Vashti McCollum, " an avowed atheist," to quote Mr. Justice Jackson, brought suit against the program being conducted in Champaign, Illinois. The program was upheld both in the Circuit Court of Champaign County and by the Illinois Supreme Court. An appeal to the United States Supreme Court resulted in an eight-to-one decision against the plan on the grounds that the use of the public school system's buildings and machinery constituted a violation of the First Amendment. The high court, however, did not ban all released time programs nor the right of pupil excusal for religious purposes. It did say that the use of the

[9] California, Indiana, Iowa, Kentucky, Maine, Massachusetts, Minnesota, New York, Oregon, Pennsylvania, South Dakota, Virginia, Hawaii, and the Philippine Islands, the latter continuing the act under its independent status.

public school system to aid in the teaching of sectarian religion was unconstitutional.

About the same time a number of other suits were brought against the program in various parts of the country. A suit against the Chicago program, which did not make use of school buildings or other forms of public school aid, was decided in favor of the program, both in the Superior Court of Cook County and in the Illinois Supreme Court. An opposition suit begun in Los Angeles was won by the friends of the program in the courts of California. Local suits in Easton, Pennsylvania; in St. Louis, Missouri; in Hutchinson, Kansas, and elsewhere were decided against the program, but were not carried to courts of higher jurisdiction in view of impending suits in the state of New York, which it was expected would give a better test of the legal issue.

A few months after the Supreme Court's decision in the Champaign case, suit was entered, again by the American Free Thinkers Society, against the New York City program and the constitutionality of the state's released time act. The New York Supreme Court (lowest court) upheld the program. When the case came up for hearing in the New York Court of Appeals (highest court), the opposition withdrew its suit.

About the same time that this case was started, another suit was entered against the program in Brooklyn, this time by persons and agencies who disavowed the non-religious views of the Free Thinkers group.[10] The bringers of this suit were Tessim Zorach and Esta Gluck, parents of public school children who " regularly attend[ed] Protestant Episcopal or Jewish schools for religious instruction at times other than the hours in which public schools are in session."

[10] See later section in this chapter, "Attitudes of Other Groups."

They were aided by various organizations which had opposed the weekday church school held on school time, some of them having filed " amici curiae " briefs in the Champaign and the New York City case just mentioned. Again the New York Supreme Court (lowest court) upheld the weekday program; the Appellate Division (intermediate court) confirmed the previous judgment; the Court of Appeals (highest court), by a six to one vote, sustained the lower courts and declared the program legally valid. In the appeal of the case to the Supreme Court of the United States, the weekday church school program again was given a national test. This time the high court on April 28, 1952, by a vote of six to three upheld the New York law and program, which was operated outside of school buildings and free from public school machinery.

This decision is a momentous one, not only for the cause of weekday religious education on school time, but for religion in America generally. Among the several significant statements of the Court we find these: " We are a religious people whose institutions presuppose a Supreme Being. . . . When the state encourages religious instruction or cooperates with religious authorities by adjusting the schedule of public events to sectarian needs, it follows the best of our traditions." In this opinion of our highest court the weekday church school has won its legal charter.

THE DENOMINATIONS TAKE NOTICE

Because the weekday church school movement has been a grass roots project, originating and developed in local communities by clerical, educational, and lay citizen groups generally, rather than being planned by national ecclesiastical leaders, the Protestant denominations as such have only slowly and more recently taken notice of it. Also, because of the ecumenical and co-operative character of the program in most of the communities, the denominational Christian education boards have had less occasion to be concerned with it and have been willing to let state and national inter-denominational agencies undertake the responsibility for its direction. Nor can it be said that any one Protestant group has taken the lead in promoting the program, although some have taken more interest in it than others. When, however, it seemed, in the light of the McCollum case decision, that there was a possibility of losing entirely the right of pupil excusal for religious education, the highest denominational educational authorities became thoroughly aroused. Resolutions of endorsement and pledges of support were passed by the national governing bodies of six major denominations and the Christian education leaders of others took firm stands in behalf of the new type of church school. The winning of the Zorach case having given the movement a clear title, the denominational adoption and more extensive use of the program is now assured.[11]

ATTITUDES OF OTHER GROUPS

This new school of religion could not very well pass unnoticed by other religious groups. When the survey sponsored by the Religious Education Association was made in 1921–22, only three or four of the 324 centers discovered showed teaching programs under the auspices of the Roman Catholic Church. A high educational leader of this Church wrote an article, which appeared in the *Catholic World*, in June, 1922, which was titled "A Protestant Experiment in

[11] See the statement made by Protestant Christian education leaders, "We Believe in the Weekday Church School," at the end of Chapter X.

Religious Education." The substance of the article was that his church would watch the development of this new agency of religious education with great interest. During the first two decades of the movement there was relatively little participation in it by Roman Catholics. However, their educational leaders studied the program carefully, with the result that they saw in it a valuable teaching agency supplementing their parochial school program and particularly helpful in reaching the unreached boys and girls of their constituency, just as has been the case with Protestants. As a consequence, in the last two decades there has been wide acceptance of the weekday church school by this group, just as it has made use of the vacation church school, another Protestant experiment.

Certain other religious groups, not co-operating in the Protestant church councils — the Church of Jesus Christ of Latter Day Saints, the Christian Scientists, the Missouri Synod Lutherans and others — have taken a great interest in the possibilities of weekday church schools and have organized their churches to operate classes. To give an example of the widespread interest of Protestants generally in the program, it can be reported that in one of the larger city co-operative weekday church school systems,[12] children representing one hundred and twelve different religious bodies are enrolled!

On the other hand, there are a few religious groups which have had less interest in this program, some of whom have vigorously opposed its use by other groups. Among these opposition groups are large numbers of Jewish leaders and organizations, Seventh Day Adventists, and Unitarians, and in addition some individual clergymen and laymen within

[12] Indianapolis, Indiana.

the favoring Protestant denominations. The opposition by these religious groups and individuals does not mean opposition to religious education. This cannot be said of those atheistic and free-thinker groups, who spearheaded the legal battles to deny the right of excusal for religious education. Now that the shadow of illegality has been dispelled, we are confident that much of the opposition will cease and there will be acceptance and use of the program by many within the previously opposing or on-the-fence church groups.

HARDER TESTS AHEAD

The weekday church school has been tested by over forty years of growth and expansion. It has been studied and appraised by many educational leaders. It has won positive legal confirmation. Its firm rootage and indigenous nature have made it, to quote Mr. Justice Reed's words in the McCollum decision, one of those " practices embedded in our society by many years of experience." But the harder tests lie ahead. These are: first, the test which comes to those who are responsible for establishing or continuing *local* weekday church school systems; and second, the test of wholehearted acceptance and support by our denominations *nationally*. It will be the purpose of the remaining chapters of this book to set forth the procedures to be followed to guarantee the successful passing of these tests.

Chapter III

Organizing a Local System

SUPPOSE there is a desire on the part of local persons —
ministers, lay church leaders, public schoolmen, or others
— to consider the establishment of a weekday church school
system to meet the needs and achieve the goals described in
Chapter I. What should such a group do? A brief and
general answer to this question includes these steps:

First, a thorough education of the local community,
including members of all religious groups, parents, public
school workers, and others;

Second, where there is no council of churches or Christian
education, the organization of a sponsoring agency representative of the Protestant and other churches which may
desire to set up a co-operative system of weekday religious
education;

Third, the working out by the sponsoring agency —
council of churches or council of weekday religious education — of a detailed plan of operation which will be effective
and permanent.

In developing this plan there must be careful consideration
of many factors, particularly financial support, an adequate
curriculum, and a competent staff of teachers and leaders.
Each of these three latter items will be treated separately in a

later chapter. Other important organizational matters will be treated in this chapter.

The very first point in " A Ten Point Platform for Weekday Church Schools " has been " a year of planning before launching the program."[1] Good educational procedure, confirmed by long experience with this new type of school of religion, more than justifies this admonition. As will be seen from our previous and later descriptions, this type of church school is different in several ways from other agencies of religious education. It must be planned rightly; otherwise it will be a sorry failure.

Probably the most important and fruitful means of learning about weekday schools are correspondence with and visitation of successful weekday systems. With the first-hand knowledge thus gained a number of local meetings should be planned with addresses, discussions, and exhibits, including audio-visual presentations. Persons particularly informed regarding this type of program should be invited to counsel with local leaders and groups — denominational and state council staff members, public school leaders who have had successful experience with the program, and also the directors of established and well-administered weekday systems.

In this planning stage the community at large and particularly the responsible leaders of the religious groups should become conversant with literature describing the program under consideration. Only as the community as a whole and these responsible persons are well informed, will the project get off to a good start and have a sound basis of per-

[1] *Remember the Weekday to Teach Religion Thereon*, p. 16.

manent support. Service bulletins and pamphlets and a bibliography may be secured from the National Council of Churches and most denominational and state council headquarters. Numerous articles have appeared in recent years in denominational magazines and in the *International Journal of Religious Education* and *Religious Education*. Included in the Standard Leadership Curriculum of the National Council of Churches is Course 612b, "Administering the Weekday Church School," for which this volume has been prepared as a study text. Wherever possible, this training course should be taken by all those persons who are interested in the proposed program and those who are to be the leaders in it.

As this first stage of educational preparation proceeds, the framework of a program will begin to emerge. It should be checked carefully with the patterns and experience of good weekday religious education, particularly with *Standards for Weekday Church Schools*, available from the National Council of Churches, and with the recommendations to be made in this and later chapters.

INTER-FAITH CO-OPERATION

In most communities, where there are public school pupils of other major faiths than those commonly grouped as Protestant, it is highly desirable to have some kind of an inter-faith or co-ordinating committee. While in practically all such situations each major faith group will set up its own curriculum and teaching program, there is much need for and value in a high degree of co-operation. To sell the total community on the program it should be clearly evident that all or a large portion of the religious forces want and will support it. In relations with public school officials a united religious approach is, in all fairness to them, to be expected.

There are a number of things which such an inter-faith agency can and should do in behalf of the entire religious constituency. The dates for beginning and ending the programs within the school year should be agreed upon mutually. The time schedule of excusal should be the same for all groups of children. Common agreement as to religious educational standards will greatly aid each of the programs. It is customary in many communities for such a committee to prepare and use a common " request for excusal " card. In some instances a united publicity and promotional approach to the community has been made and a common interpretive leaflet has been prepared and used. In the light of these and other ways of working together, this representative agency of the several faith groups should meet frequently, both before and during the school year.[2]

A REPRESENTATIVE PROTESTANT COUNCIL

If there is a council of churches or council of Christian education in the community, the sponsoring group for the weekday program should be a part of, or closely related to, such a council. If there is no such council, then a council for weekday religious education should be organized, and assume the working functions which we shall describe. Its membership should include various persons — clergymen, Christian lay leaders, parents, P.-T.A. officers and members, leaders of the community character-building agencies, public school workers unofficially, and other interested and religious-minded citizens. So far as possible, these council members should be elected by the governing bodies of the

[2] See also " Relations With Other Faiths," p. 115.

local churches and chosen from their membership on a representative basis.

It cannot be too strongly emphasized that a successful system of weekday religious education must have a broadly based, a continuing, and an alert sponsoring agency. A weekday religious education committee, council, or board must not be limited in membership and sponsorship to a ministerial association, a council of church women, or other single agency of the total church program. While the initial discussion of such a program and the wholehearted support of the project by such a limited group is to be welcomed, its sound development and continuous undergirding require a sponsorship widely representative of the total Protestant church life — both lay persons and clergy, men and women, educators, parents, and citizens.

For this reason, even where there is an active council of churches or council of Christian education, it may be helpful to enlist the interest of a large group of persons in the weekday program. These persons may constitute an advisory council or weekday church school fellowship. It may meet once or twice a year to review the program, make suggestions for its improvement, and furnish informed community support for it. Such an advisory group may well have an executive committee whose membership is identical with or related to the church council's committee on weekday religious education or committee on Christian education.

A PLAN OF OPERATION

A well-organized plan of operation, functioning through an administrative board and special committees, will require careful planning with respect to a number of items, including the type of local program, the number of grades and centers to be included, pupil excusal and enrollment, the time schedule, housing places for classes, equipment and servicing. These particular jobs will be discussed in the sections which follow.

SINGLY OR IN CO-OPERATION?

One of the most significant decisions which must be made is whether the proposed weekday church school system is to be one in which each church teaches its own children, or whether all or most of the co-operating churches will pool their resources and establish a community system of instruction. There are good arguments for each type.

When each individual church undertakes to set up a weekday teaching program of its own, there are the advantages of emphasizing its particular doctrines, using its own curriculum materials, employing teachers of its own persuasion, and having the project considered as one of its own church activities. A minority of the local weekday church school systems are of this type.

The large majority of the systems are inter-church in type, systems in which there are unified organizations, common curriculum plans, teachers chosen without respect to particular denominational relationship, meeting places selected on the bases of suitability and nearness to the public school, common budgets and shared responsibility for raising them. The numerical preponderance of this co-operative type of weekday system is a tribute to pioneering in ecumenicity demonstrated by the movement. Over against the values which the advocates of the single church type of program emphasize, the inter-church system has these: greater efficiency in operation; the need for fewer and usually better trained teachers; much less divisiveness, which appeals to progressive church leaders, public school leaders, and parents generally; a lower cost per pupil; and, most significant of all, the reaching of a very much larger proportion of un-churched children — averaging twenty-five per cent for the program as a whole and reaching over the fifty per cent mark in the " inner city " and industrial areas of some of our great metropolitan centers.

In communities where there are churches strongly in favor of the individual church type of program, the wisest policy is not to attempt to pressure them to join in a common teaching program, but to respect their desires in the hope that they will join later after the co-operative pattern has demonstrated its values. By the same token, the fact that such churches desire to " go it alone " should not mean that all the other churches should not operate a co-operative system.

HOW MANY GRADES AND CENTERS?

Another important decision on the part of the sponsoring agency is the number of grades to be included in the program. In the earlier years overly ambitious advocates advised a program reaching from the kindergarten through Grade VIII and often through the senior high school. While a few such programs seemed to be successful, experience has indicated the undesirability of such an extensive program as an initial venture. Two, or three, or four grades are about all that a new system can care for effectively or for which it can raise the necessary budget.

It is the usual practice to group the pupils in the same classes or grades which they attend in the public school. Sometimes it may be necessary to enroll pupils from two or more public school grades to make a reasonable-sized church school class. This is one of the practices which the individual church program is of necessity forced to adopt. Occasionally some of the better weekday church school systems have had to set up two church school classes for the pupils from one public school grade in order to hold to the standards of good teaching.

Experience has also shown that, in a large city, and sometimes in a smaller place, it is unwise to attempt to operate a weekday program in all areas at the start. It is preferable to initiate work in a few pilot centers, maintaining these on a high educational level, then gradually expanding the program as successful meeting of the problems involved and an increased budget warrant its extension.

PUPIL EXCUSAL AND ENROLLMENT

An early step in starting a weekday church school program is arranging for the excusal of pupils. As in the case of excusing pupils for any worthy reason, it is both legally and educationally necessary to have the signed request of the parent or guardian of the child. Most weekday systems provide duplicate card forms for this purpose. One of these is filed with the public school authorities and the other becomes the registration record of the weekday church school.

In order that a high percentage of public school pupils may be secured for the weekday religious education program, a thorough house-to-house canvass of the area represented in the public school constituency must be made. Pupil enrollments must not be secured in the public school buildings, nor can public school workers in their official capacities assist in the registration of pupils, although they can be of service outside of school hours and their school buildings. Other practical and legal methods of securing a high percentage of the public school enrollment include canvassing pupils in Sunday and vacation church schools, asking the help of P.-T. A. members, and securing names of new families from Welcome Wagon hostesses and chambers of commerce.

One question frequently asked is: should a weekday program be undertaken for a relatively small number of pupils? "If some of the groups have not had opportunity to consider the plan, other groups should not proceed hastily. The plan succeeds to the extent that the whole community is well informed and sympathetic. On the other hand, after a reasonable time for consideration, it is not fair for those not desiring to use the plan to oppose others wishing to do so."[3]

Additional factors must also be weighed: (1) The Supreme Court decision in the Zorach case stresses the variety of our religious needs and treats *all* excusals for religious purposes as of the same character, "whether . . . occasionally for a few students, regularly for one, or pursuant to a systematized program designed to meet the needs of all the students." In accordance with this legal right, pupils of various faiths now absent themselves for their particular religious needs. (2) The legal right, however, must be balanced by consideration for the public school system, which obligates religious groups to co-operate and work for the largest possible enrollment in the weekday church school program. (3) Whether the churches of a community are united in the establishment of a program or not, some groups or individual churches are bound to take advantage of this right of excusal, even though others may not do so. It thus behooves our Protestant churches

[3] *Remember the Weekday to Teach Religion Thereon*, p. 13.

and local church councils to become thoroughly conversant with the nature of a weekday church school program, so as to make the best possible decision in the light of the total community situation at the time.

It is important and highly desirable that regular reports of children attending weekday church school classes be made by the weekday church school teachers to the public school authorities. Some of the opponents of this type of religious school have objected to this practice on the grounds of its alleged illegality, but this procedure received the forthright approval of the Supreme Court in the Zorach case decision. In cases of repeated truancy or unexcused absence from the weekday church school classes, it is the rule of most weekday systems to ask the parents to cancel their excusal request and to deny the admission of such pupils to the weekday church school classes.

THE TIME SCHEDULE

There are several questions which come under this heading. One of these is whether use should be made of the " released time " principle or whether the " dismissed time " plan be followed. In the former case, only those pupils are excused whose parents request it; all other pupils remain in the public school for whatever optional or individually desirable activity is provided for them, with the understanding that such activity is not to be competitive in character with the religious education program. Thus, as the Supreme Court recommended, " the teacher . . . co-operates in a religious education program to the extent of making it possible for her students to participate in it."

By " dismissed time " is meant the official closing of all the public school grades involved one or more hours per week, usually the last hour of some one day. This leaves it to the child's interest or his parent's powers of persuasiveness as to whether he will attend religious education classes or engage in play or other activities. Psychologically and practically " dismissed time " becomes out-of-school time. It has not worked and very few communities have adopted it.[4] If consistently applied to all pupil excusals for a religious need, it would wreck the public school teaching schedule, for it would mean that, whenever some of the pupils are excused for *their* particular religious need, at any time during the day or week, all other pupils of whatever faith or none, should be dismissed at the same time. The high court saw no need for suggesting this type of program, but endorsed the released time principle as the legally valid and practicable answer to the child's religious needs.

A far-reaching decision to be made by the sponsoring agency and the co-operating public school authorities is whether the program will make use of a staggered or simultaneous schedule of excusal and class teaching. The latter schedule means that all the children whose parents so request it are excused at the same time. The former means that children of the several grades are excused at different times, so that all through the day and week classes in religion are meeting. Only to the degree that the teaching schedule for the classes in religion is thus distributed is it possible to make use of full-time, professionally trained teachers of religion. Where there is little or no distributing of the teaching schedule, a large number of teachers is required, making the task of securing them, training them, and

[4] The " Statement of Policy Regarding Weekday Religious Education " of the Division of Christian Education of the National Council of Churches asserts: " Weekday hours outside of those commonly devoted to formal education are not satisfactory. . . . Religion is of sufficient importance to justify a place in the hours of formal education."

keeping them on the job an heroic and almost impossible one, to say nothing of the irregular quality of the teaching done.

Where the teaching schedule must be limited to one or a very few periods a week, the situation can be greatly helped by such provisions as these: (1) A well-selected and hard-working personnel committee should be on the job to secure the names of able teachers and arrange for their employment. (2) A set of reasonable standards for teachers should be adopted and followed. (3) A continuous program of teacher training should be a part of the weekday system. (4) One or more good supervisors should be employed as helping teachers. (5) Provision should be made for payment for teaching, using the public school substitute-teacher scale as a guide. (6) An *esprit de corps* and loyalty among the teachers should be developed by recognizing their service in various ways and giving them the assistance they need to do good work.

How much time per week is given to each weekday church school class? Usually one hour, sometimes two. The term "hour" is often interpreted as a period, which may be as short as a half hour or as long as an hour and a quarter. A portion of this time is taken in going to and returning from the church or other place of instruction, unless the class period is at the beginning or end of the morning or afternoon session of the public school. In this case the going or returning time is taken from the child's free time, which allows a longer period for actual class work.

HOUSING THE CLASSES

"The building which houses the weekday church school classes should provide the best possible facilities for worship, study and physical comfort," say the *Standards for Week-*

day Church Schools.[5] In meeting these standards the sponsoring agency will have to consider lighting, heating, ventilation, size of room, its attractiveness, clothes racks, and toilet facilities — in fact many things which are important in providing the setting for good teaching. It is significant that our better weekday systems, in arranging with local churches or other agencies for the use of their buildings, insist upon considering just such matters.

It is now accepted that weekday church school classes held during school hours should not meet in public school classrooms, even where local school authorities invite the classes in religion to do so. This was clearly stated in the McCollum decision and definitely reaffirmed in the Zorach decision. Most of the communities in which this was formerly the practice, about forty per cent of the total prior to the McCollum decision, have ceased to do so, with the result that two years later the number had shrunk to only fifteen per cent. This means that in most communities the use of churches as meeting places has become standard procedure. In fact, most church leaders believe that churches with adequate educational facilities furnish a more desirable atmosphere for these classes.

One major difficulty, however, with reference to holding classes in churches is that they are not always located near the public schools from which the children are excused. This means a shortening of the teaching time available. To meet this problem, various weekday systems have made other plans. Some have devised a system of transportation, using buses or private cars. Many of the systems, both where the children walk to and from the church or are

[5] See page 13 of booklet.

transported, have set up an escort system. Parents and other persons volunteer for this special service.

A number of weekday systems, where the churches are not conveniently located, have made use of other buildings located near the schools — libraries, social centers, and even garages! A considerable number hold classes in nearby homes — a practice which, in spite of some inconveniences, is not without its definite values. In a few cases small chapels have been built adjacent to the public school. The outstanding example of erecting special buildings for housing weekday classes is that of the Church of Jesus Christ of Latter Day Saints. This church has built one hundred and sixteen such religious education plants close by the public schools from which the pupils are excused on a staggered time schedule.

One of the most ingenious and effective answers to the housing problem, where the churches are located at a distance, is the use of " mobile classrooms." These specially built and educationally equipped trailers are being increasingly used. They are hauled from one school location to another and parked on the street or a nearby lot. Many of them make better teaching places than do some church rooms. Their use has also enabled the weekday systems using them to conduct classes in new areas of the community in which churches have not been erected. Quite aside from their usefulness in furnishing classroom space, these mobile classrooms are a symbol of the determination of these communities to have weekday religious education in spite of the difficulties involved.

EQUIPMENT AND SERVICES

As in the case of any good educational program, weekday church schools not only need adequate housing facilities but the right equipment. A visit to a modern public school will amaze those whose recollections can go back to the " little red schoolhouse." Churches, too, have found that, for good weekday church school teaching, they must have furniture, literature, and supplies commensurate with those found in our fine public schools. We can mention only a few items, which should suggest others: blackboards, tables and chairs, filing cabinets, a piano, maps, flat pictures and other visual aids, record players and records, writing materials, the usual " activities " materials and, of course, Bibles and the best curriculum materials for both the pupils and the teacher. These latter will be treated in the next chapter.

The proper servicing of the classroom is also important. The right arrangement of the equipment and other facilities and the orderliness and cleanliness of the room require regular custodial service, which in most cases should not be expected of the teacher if her teaching effectiveness is not to be impaired.

We have sketched only some of the matters that should be seriously considered by the agency which sponsors a weekday church school program. The proper attention to these and other items spells success. Inattention spells failure, as some weekday systems have discovered to their great regret. No sponsoring agency should fail to appreciate the responsibility which it accepts in setting up a local weekday church school program.

Chapter IV

Planning the Curriculum

What do they teach in weekday church schools?"
This is one of the first questions asked by those whose interest
is aroused but who have little knowledge of the program.
Another frequent question, sometimes phrased as a comment
of surprise, is: " Can you use the same courses with children
who belong to different churches?" The answer to the latter
query is: " Yes, this is one of the unique and remarkable
features of the community type of weekday church school."
Widespread experience has shown that the selection and
use of curriculum materials is not one of the more troubling
problems of this kind of school, but one of the less difficult.

Nevertheless, it must not be assumed that success comes
about without much effort and careful planning. The
strength of an inter-church weekday church school system
and its effective use of a common course of study are due
both to the ecumenical spirit which pervades the movement
as a whole and to the concern which local organizers have
for the adoption of a satisfactory curriculum. The importance which this has in the minds of local planners is
evidenced by the fact that there are probably more inquiries
sent to the office of the National Council of Churches and the
offices of denominations and state councils asking for cur-

riculum help than for any other single item in the weekday program. This is an evidence of good judgment, if the inquiry comes early in the consideration of a prospective program. Unfortunately, it sometimes comes as a late afterthought, and the hoped-for program either has to be delayed or proceeds with a curriculum carelessly put together.

How then should the serious-minded sponsoring agency go about providing a good course of study?

A CURRICULUM COMMITTEE

A committee on curriculum is one of the necessary working groups recommended in a later chapter. Its members should be carefully selected on the basis of their concern and experience with curriculum matters. It should include one or more ministers, but not be predominantly ministerial in its make-up. A trained and competent director of religious education should be one of the members. It should have lay representation, especially from the parents' groups in the community. One or more persons working with the community's character-building agencies can make a special contribution here. It is particularly valuable to have at least one of the public school staff (on a personal rather than an official basis) on this committee. If possible it should be the person who has most to do with curriculum planning in the public school. Such a person can be of invaluable help. The weekday church school system's director, supervisor, or head teacher should be a member ex-officio, for his or her experience ought not to be overlooked.

THE COMMITTEE AT WORK

The first thing the committee should do is to gather all the materials and other help it can on the problem. This means sending for bulletins and catalogs describing available courses and also samples of these courses. These helps can be secured from the office of the National Council of Churches, from denominational boards of Christian education, and in some cases from the state councils of churches, or the larger city councils. It will be of great advantage if the curriculum plan of the local public school system for the grades from which pupils are to be excused is secured for examination. Of great value, both for its contribution to the knowledge of how a successful weekday system as a whole operates and for the way in which its curriculum functions, is a visit to one or more places where a good program is in operation. Needless to say, all these materials and reports of observations made should be studied with painstaking care by the curriculum committee.

Early in its work the committee should decide on the aims and purposes of the prospective teaching program. It should be familiar with the objectives of Christian education as a whole and the particular contributions which the new weekday church school may be expected to make to them. It will consult parents, Sunday and vacation church school workers, pastors of churches, directors of religious education, religious-minded public school leaders and others to discover what emphasis or emphases ought to be given in the weekday church school curriculum. There are also other important factors to be considered as indicated by this significant quotation from a weekday church school curriculum bulletin:

HOW TO SELECT A COURSE

In choosing a course for any age group in a weekday church school, the committee should in each case consider:

The Children

Their needs, interests, abilities and opportunities. This means a frank facing of the maturity of the children in a given class. Are they advanced, average or retarded for their years? Have they had wide or limited experiences with books, travel and with educated adults? Such questions as these might help to determine whether a particular textbook should be used in a particular grade.

Their education received from other sources. The weekday curriculum committee must take into account the courses of study which the children have been following in their Sunday church school and vacation church school programs. Great care needs to be exercised lest texts be chosen and used in a weekday church school, for example, which some of the cooperating churches are using in these other church schools.

The Teachers

Their training and experience. If their background is limited, the committee would do well to choose a course which those with less training can use. The grade placement of a course will be determined in part by the ability of the teacher. For example, one teacher will be able to use successfully a course marked " Sixth Grade " with boys and girls in grade five of the public school. Another teacher might have greater success if he used a fourth grade course with the same age group.

Their time for preparation and the resources available. Courses will not " teach themselves." It is true, however, that some will require less intensive study than others. Some contain a general outline or merely basic source materials on the expectation that the teacher will fill in the enrichment material after reading and research. Such courses should be selected only for the use of teachers who have time and opportunity for this.

Space and Time Available for the
Weekday Church School

Place of meeting. Some courses may be taught in a room which is small and limited in equipment, while others by their very nature demand a spacious room and certain basic equipment.

The length of the period. A forty-five minute teaching period once a week for twenty-five weeks means ten or twelve session plans are sufficient. Two periods would be necessary in order to round out one complete session plan and give variety of activity. On the other hand, an hour or more per week allows for a much longer and more extensive course.[1]

The problem of choosing courses for a curriculum acceptable to a number of different church groups sponsoring the weekday system is not easy, although, as we have said, there has been remarkable success at this point. The committee should try to be as objective as possible and formulate for itself a set of standards by which it will seek to measure prospective courses. This will help in avoiding a policy of " I'll include your (denominational) course, if you'll include mine." It is expected that no course chosen will contain materials reflecting on the sincerity, particular doctrines or practices of the co-operating churches. The same principle should hold with reference to those of other church groups, who may not be included in the common teaching program.

WHAT IS A GOOD COURSE?

As an aid to curriculum committees in evaluating courses being examined, the following list of questions is quoted from a form prepared and used by the Committee on Week-

[1] *Choosing a Course of Study for Your Weekday Church School,* pp. 3-4. (Out of print.)

day Religious Education for judging weekday church school texts:

1. Are its purposes and content as a whole in harmony with the area of study for which it was selected?
2. Is it suitable for the grades for which it is proposed?
3. Is this book up to date in viewpoint, content, and procedure?
4. Is it Christian in purpose and content?

   Note: Each text will not be concerned with all of these objectives, but should fulfill those with which it is concerned. Check only points which apply to this text.

   a. Does it have an adequate concept of God?
   b. Does it present an idea of Jesus that will challenge children to be loyal to him?
   c. Will it guide boys and girls in developing Christlike character?
   d. Does it help children develop attitudes toward the social order which embody clear concepts of the fatherhood of God and the brotherhood of man? Would it challenge children to put these concepts into practice?
   e. Does it foster in the child a desire to identify himself with the on-going work of the church?
   f. Does it help children find vital resources for living in the Bible and other elements of the Christian heritage (such as hymns, art, music, etc.)?
   g. Does it lead children to have a Christian interpretation of the universe?
   h. Does it foster Christian ideals of life in the family?

5. Is it interdenominational in its viewpoint?

6. Does it adequately and fairly represent other racial, cultural, and religious groups when it refers to them in the course?
7. Does it give sufficient guidance for teachers' preparation of session plans?
8. Does the text provide for adequate pupil participation in plans and procedures, such as discussion, dramatization, excursions, and creative activities?
9. Does the text have adequate teacher and pupil resources such as stories, poems, hymns, audio-visual materials, and directions for activities suggested in the session plans?
10. Does the text make evident its relationship to the child's experience in home, school, and church?
11. Is the text usable or adaptable within the time limit and classroom facilities provided in the typical situation?
12. Is the format of the pupil's book attractive?
13. Is the pupil material a suitable and adequate resource for his work and study?[2]

HOMEMADE COURSES

In the earlier years of the weekday church school development it was the practice for local systems to prepare their own courses. In practically all cases these materials were mimeographed outlines for the teacher's guidance and the pupil's material (if any) was a brief story or work sheet of some kind. As time passed and more satisfactory materials were produced by various agencies, the use of these homemade courses has tended to disappear. In the competitive and sifting process, several of the better locally produced curricula have survived and are used in areas outside of that for which they were originally produced.

[2] See also *A Guide for Curriculum in Christian Education* (National Council of Churches).

The reasons why these local materials were first developed include these: There was a real need for them, for there was a scarcity of courses which could be used for weekday church school classes. They usually cost less, for they were somewhat brief and were put out in mimeographed form. They represented local interest, pride, and creativity. They were pitched to local needs and teaching levels.

The attitude of the Division of Christian Education of the National Council of Churches toward locally produced courses is found in a statement in *Standards for Weekday Church Schools:* " The use of independent and locally developed curriculum materials in the weekday church school field is generally not advised." On the other hand, it should be said that this does not close the door to their use provided they meet the acceptable educational standards and the practical needs of local situations. It is the policy of those who are planning and producing the Co-operative Texts for weekday schools to have these win their way through their quality and proven suitability for use. Our next section will describe these courses.

THE CO-OPERATIVE SERIES

The Co-operative Weekday Church School Series of texts for use in weekday programs is meeting a long-standing and increasing need felt by local weekday church school systems. These materials are created and issued by an organization known as the Co-operative Publication Association, representing the publishing houses of those denominations belonging to the National Council of Churches.

The procedure for the production of these weekday texts begins with the development of outlines for courses which are needed by local weekday church schools. These outlines, or detailed descriptions of courses, are the product of the Committee on the Graded Series of the National Council of Churches. These descriptions, after receiving the approval of the denominations and the Council's Commission on General Christian Education, are made available for use by the co-operating denominations.

In pursuance of this practice the Co-operative Publication Association, on the advice of its special Committee on Weekday Texts, selects the courses for which materials are most immediately needed, names writers to prepare texts (both for pupil use and for teacher guidance), and sets up procedures for editorial supervision and publication. Throughout the time of preparation the projected materials have the constructive criticisms of the special committee, the several denominational editors, and other specialists in weekday work.

Thus the denominations " pool their resources " and plan, write, and publish together guidance material and courses for the weekday church schools. These materials, to quote with approval the descriptive brochure of the Association,[3] are " distinctly and uniquely religious, rich in Biblical content, well rounded in regard to the essentials of the Christian faith, well written, and planned with a variety of materials emphasizing: *The Bible, The Church, Christian Living, God's World.*"

As a part of this text preparation process, competent local weekday teachers are invited to make use of the descriptive outlines of prospective courses, before they are developed into texts. Sometimes one outline will be tried out by weekday teachers in several local systems. From this experimental

[3] Send for a copy of the latest edition to the Department of Weekday Religious Education, National Council of Churches.

use of outlines comes much valuable help for the person chosen to write the course. Also through this process the person best qualified to become the text writer is often discovered. In some cases the preliminary manuscript is also used experimentally before being put in final form for publication. Thus the local weekday systems and their teachers are sharing increasingly in creative curriculum development, both to the satisfaction of those who shy away from office-made materials and to the undoubted improvement of weekday church school courses.

CURRICULUM INTEGRATION

" Weekday church schools are not substitutes for any other educational agency of the church. They are supplementary and complementary to them. Each agency has its unique contribution to a total, multiple program of Christian education. It is important, therefore, that both local church and community boards of Christian education organize the curriculum of each agency, including that of the weekday church schools, so as to bring about the highest possible degree of correlation and integration of the total teaching program." [4]

It is very difficult, if not impossible, to produce weekday curriculum materials at the national level of such a character that, even if all weekday systems were to use the Co-operative Texts, for example, these could be correlated with locally used Sunday or vacation church school texts. There are too many variations among the many denominational courses, even between courses used by the churches of the same denomination, to hope for such an achievement. Some

[4] *Standards for Weekday Church Schools*, p. 16.

degree of correlation and integration, however, is possible within the local community.

There are certain courses which obviously belong to a local church curriculum and should not be included in a co-operative weekday church school curriculum. These are doctrinal courses; denominational and local church history, polity, and practice; denominational missionary and social service programs; courses in denominational church worship; and courses leading to church membership and personal commitment.

On the other hand, there are many fruitful opportunities to stress, in the weekday curriculum offerings, courses which are particularly suggested by its inter-church nature — courses stressing ecumenicity; the programs and activities of local, state, national, and world councils of churches; and comparative religions — which can be introduced a bit more easily in a co-operative church school meeting on the weekday.

A considerable amount of correlation can be done, not so much through the choice of a particular course, as through the work of the teacher regardless of the course being pursued. The imaginative teacher, more or less familiar with the courses being used in the local churches with which her pupils are connected, can relate her teaching to that which the pupils are receiving there. This is an added reason for the use of full-time, trained teachers, for they can make it their business to become familiar with what is being taught the children elsewhere.

There are definite possibilities for correlation of the teaching in a weekday church school with the teaching being done in the public schools from which the pupils are excused. The public school curriculum is fairly well standardized so that its contents, though not always the order of their use, are much the same throughout the nation. All the children in the weekday church school are also enrolled in the public school. The trained weekday religious education teacher, in many cases having had public school teaching experience, is quite familiar with the public school curriculum or can easily become so. For such teachers a high degree of correlation, where it is desired, is easily attainable.

The way in which this works is illustrated by this example: In a certain weekday church school system the teacher learned that, in the public school, her pupils were to study early colonial history. In the light of this fact, she planned a weekday church school project of studying early colonial churches. In both the public school and weekday church school classes, the knowledge each class acquired was mutually enriching and was shared frequently with the other. An interesting article describing the project was happily titled, " Two Helpings of History, Please! " [5]

It is of the utmost importance that the weekday church school program should not be considered as a substitute for home training in religion. Rather there should be the closest co-operation between the two agencies. Good weekday teachers will find it possible to relate their teaching to home experiences. In the stronger weekday systems a certain amount of the time for which the teacher is employed is expected to be used in home visitation. In one system, a total of three hundred hours was given to home contacts during the school year, much to the strengthening of the teaching program and the solving of pupil and home problems.[6]

[5] Landers, Ethna, *International Journal of Religious Education.*
[6] See also pages 109-111.

We close this chapter with a plea that weekday church school teachers be encouraged to make the greatest possible use of their curriculum materials. It is trite but true to say that a course is more than a text, more than studying and talking *about* Jesus' life and way. The writers of the pupils' and teachers' books intend that the pupil activities suggested should be an integral part of the course. Too frequently these are ignored or short-cut in favor of " imparting knowledge " because " there is so little time." It is difficult, to be sure, to have weekday church school classes or individual pupils do things or go places outside of the period when they are in class. But this is occasionally possible, as some weekday teachers can testify. And many worthwhile activities are possible within the class period.

What are the kinds of " red letter " activities which are usually to be found in good weekday church school courses and which should not be overlooked? Many teachers have given their classes long-remembered experiences through a visit to the church or synagogue of another religious group, or to a religious shrine, an art gallery, or church headquarters. Similar trips to a museum, mission, settlement house, or court have possibilities. Enlarging experiences can be had within the classroom and in class time — visits from religious leaders, Christian officeholders, or children from another religious group. A wide range of audio and visual presentations are available to enrich the course units or to use as an occasional alternative program when there is good reason for doing so. Dramatic presentations aid in vivifying the lessons. Making gifts for others—the aged and shut-ins, children who are sick or under institutional care, those of other races and religious groups — furnish outlets for creativity and kindliness. Frequently weekday classes have engaged in service projects such as a " Mitten Tree " for European children, heifer projects, and Bibles for Korea. Other fruitful projects include sending letters of encouragement to hard-pressed Christian and civic leaders, and Christian observances of national holidays. During the week of April 28 each year, the anniversary of the United States Supreme Court's favorable decision in the Zorach case, some weekday classes hold special observances and contribute to a fund to help bring weekday church schools to communities which do not have them.

Chapter V

The Teaching Staff

THE ASSERTION that the curriculum is ninety per cent teacher is especially true in the case of the weekday church school. Wherever any advance in pupil achievement is shown in these weekday classes as compared with other teaching agencies of the local church, more credit must be given to a higher level of teacher ability than to other factors. Not to expect such improvement would be to disavow a basic educational axiom that better trained teachers do better teaching. Foremost among the goals for the weekday church school is that of expecting its teachers to have had a training for their jobs which is equivalent to that of the public school teachers who teach the same children in the public school. While this goal has not been reached in all of the weekday church school systems, in those where it has become standard practice the results have more than justified the faith of those who chose to employ a thoroughly trained as well as a consecrated teaching staff.

A COMMITTEE ON PERSONNEL

A committee on the selection, guidance, and recognition of members of the teaching staff, in the light of the importance we have attached to the teaching factor, is one which cannot be dispensed with even in smaller weekday systems.

While the final authority in the employment of staff rests with the administrative board, the care and time which the personnel committee gives to locating and investigating candidates will go far toward guaranteeing the choice of the right worker or workers. On the personnel committee there should be such persons as ministers, directors of religious education, public school supervisors or principals (acting unofficially), officers or members of the Parent-Teacher Association, and members of church committees on Christian education.

In ways which we will discuss later in this chapter under the heading, "Finding Teachers," this committee will secure the names of persons qualified for weekday service. From such candidates it will ask for detailed information as to their education, teaching experience, religious experience, character, interests, and other matters. It will request references, with whom it will correspond. Whenever it is practicable it will arrange for personal interviews, particularly in the case of the employment of a director, supervisor, or head teacher. When it has narrowed its investigation to the choice of one person, it will recommend election by the board and will see that a contract is drawn up setting forth the duties of the teacher and of the employing council. Election to teaching service in a weekday school is usually on an annual basis.

We have indicated that guidance is also a responsibility of the personnel committee. By this we mean a reasonable and helpful oversight of the work of the teacher, particularly where there is no employed supervisor or director. There are also many things which can and should be done to assist and encourage teachers, especially when they are new to the job.

It is also wise practice for the personnel committee to see that the teachers have a real share in determining the program and policies of the school. Many weekday systems provide for installing and consecrating their teaching staff at the beginning of the school year, and also see that in other ways throughout the year the teachers are given the recognition which their position and devotion to the cause deserve.

THE GOOD TEACHER

What makes a good teacher for a weekday church school? Undoubtedly, such a teacher should have the same qualifications as good teachers in other types of schools, but with special emphasis upon religious experience and personality. To such a teacher, the term " professionally trained " means a training for a full-time Christian service to which she is utterly consecrated. This does not excuse unattractiveness in appearance or quirks of personality. It does require that she be able to work happily and harmoniously with others — church school workers, public school workers, adults and citizens generally, and of course with children.

To be trained for this type of teaching requires that the teacher should be a graduate of a standard college or training school for public school or church workers, or both, with specialization in courses in religion and religious education.

Experience — successful — is also a requirement for a good weekday church school teacher. This may be acquired in several ways — in public school work, in practice teaching in her college or training school course, or in a good Sunday or vacation church school. Beginning weekday church school teachers are advised to start their career in one of the stronger systems so that they may have the experience of learning from the master teachers which such a system affords.

Pre-service education is a must; in-service training is likewise. The good weekday teacher grows on the job. She does this by taking additional courses in summer sessions or upon sabbatical leaves, or both. Equally valuable as in-service training are the constructive guidance of a good supervisor, professional reading, visiting the classes of teachers who are known to do superior teaching, and helping in the development of improved courses for one's own weekday school.

A LOOK AT THE JOB

As a Christian vocation teaching in weekday church schools is relatively new. It is to be expected, therefore, that it has not yet been fully standardized. The best understanding of the various tasks and responsibilities will come rather by a slower process of experience than by an overhead " must." Weekday systems which have had successful experience with the selection of teachers have found it desirable, both for their own efficiency and for that of the teachers they employ, to have a clear picture of the job.

Therefore, it is recommended that the personnel committee make a job analysis of the task of the teacher. An experienced weekday supervisor suggests these matters for the consideration of the personnel committee:

1. *Type of Position.* Is the teacher to have only teaching duties or will she have certain administrative functions in addition? This practice will differ according to the size of the weekday system.

2. *Classroom Activities.* What types of experiences do you want the teacher to provide for the pupils? Should

these include Bible study, worship, discussion, hymn study, creative activities and service projects? What will be the teaching load in terms of number of classes, number of pupils, length of class periods, number of grades and of schools? If she is expected to do a certain amount of individual pupil guidance, how much time will be allowed in the schedule for this?

3. *Home Contacts.* Do you want the teacher to link the weekday program with the home through visitation, letters, reports and parent-teacher meetings? Is time designated in her schedule for making home contacts?

4. *Church Contacts.* What is to be the relation of the teacher to the churches of the community? How should she relate the weekday program to the ongoing church life of the community? In what ways should she work with the Sunday church school teachers of her pupils?

Ideas on the relation of the weekday teacher to the churches of the community vary greatly among weekday systems, and for this reason the matter should be given careful consideration. The resulting decision should be made clear to the teacher and to the pastors of the cooperating churches. Should the teacher move her membership to the local church of her choice, or would it be better if she not affiliate with any one denomination in that community? Should she be at liberty to take a regular Sunday position in one church, such as the superintendency of the junior department, or should she be free to visit all of the churches attended by her pupils and to serve each church on occasion?

5. *School Contacts.* Since the Champaign case called attention to the importance of the correct relationship between the weekday program and the public school, it is more essential than ever that the attitude of the weekday teacher to the public school teachers be defined clearly. There must be no organic connection between the two systems, and yet, because the teachers are work-

ing with the same pupils, there must be a friendly, harmonious understanding.

6. Conferences, Records and Reports. Will there be certain local, state, or national weekday conferences in which the teacher will be expected to participate? What records of pupils and of classes should the teacher keep? What types of reports should she make to the sponsoring organization and how frequently should they be made?

7. Administrative Responsibilities. If there is a full time director for the weekday system the teacher will have little to do with the administrative side of the program. However in a system with only one teacher and no other professional leadership, she probably will have to assume responsibility along with the executive committee for some of the administrative functions. These may include helping to organize the program, making arrangements for housing the classes, setting up the teaching schedule, securing the necessary equipment and supplies, getting the enrollment, building the curriculum, and improving public relations. It is important that the prospective teacher be led to understand the responsibilities she will have to assume in this area, and that she feels able and willing to undertake these functions.[1]

As further assistance to personnel committees it is urged that they study both Section I, Personnel, and the other sections of *Standards for Weekday Church Schools* together with the bulletin *A Guide for Developing a Job Analysis for Weekday Religious Education Workers,* both available from the National Council of Churches. Observation of other teachers in good weekday systems and conferences with successful teachers will also enrich the committee's background for the selection of a teacher.

[1] Longwell, Elizabeth, " When You Employ a Weekday Teacher," *International Journal of Religious Education.*

It is desirable that what is expected of a teacher, and also what is expected of the sponsoring council in turn, should be clearly understood by both and stated, at least in brief, in a written contract or letter. Having indicated what the teacher is expected to do, we may next take a look at what obligations rest upon the employing council.

Even before salary considerations is the Christian obligation to do all possible to make the teacher contented and happy in her work. Consideration, moral backing, understanding and recognition, community friendliness — all these suggest things which go far in contributing to the teacher's success.

A weekday teacher is worthy of her hire. She should have a salary as nearly equal as possible to that which other social servants of the community are paid, more specifically that of the public school teachers of the corresponding grade. Many weekday systems have set this as their standard salary.

In addition to a basic salary, with regular if not large increases, there are other items of remuneration now considered as due all workers — accident and health insurance, hospitalization and medical care, and social security payments or other pension provisions.

There are certain items of teacher expense which should be considered. Transportation to the various places of teaching should be provided. If the teacher owns a car, a proper allowance for its operation should be made. The wise council makes provision for its workers' membership in and attendance at professional group meetings — local, state, and national.

The length of the teaching year should be clearly understood, with a vacation period specified. Some weekday systems wisely employ weekday teachers on a year-round basis and use them as directors or principals of their vacation church schools. Sick leave and substitute teachers are also a part of the council's responsibility and add to the teachers' appreciation and more efficient work.

One more council responsibility: that of providing for any necessary teaching expenses such as supplies, postage, room decoration, reference materials, and special equipment. Sometimes these can be a burden on the teacher's small salary and they must not be overlooked by the council in making up its weekday budget.

WHO SHALL TEACH?

When a new weekday church school system is being projected the question immediately arises: Who shall be our teachers? This leads to further questions: Shall we employ one or more full-time, professionally trained persons, or a larger number of part-time persons with training, or depend upon volunteers? Should ministers do some or all of the teaching? The answers to these and related questions depend in part on the kind of excusal schedule to be followed in the local community, in part upon the amount of financial support for the program which can be secured, and in even larger part upon the ideals and standards which the local council has with respect to this kind of a program. Let us endeavor to reply to these questions by quoting certain relevant questions and answers given in the widely used pamphlet, *Remember the Weekday to Teach Religion Thereon*.[2]

" *Which are better, paid or volunteer teachers?* Paid teachers are greatly to be preferred, since they can be asked

[2] Published by the National Council of Churches.

to meet accepted teaching standards and to keep a regular teaching schedule and are more likely to have had and to continue in training." What we have said thus far in this chapter and throughout the volume is on the assumption that most weekday church school systems will employ full-time or part-time, trained workers. To expect those who teach in this type of school of religion which is conducted on school time to have training and experience equivalent to the teachers in the public schools is no different from expecting educational workers in home or foreign missionary work to have a high level of training and to pay them on a service vocation basis.

If the question of consecration is raised, let it be said that there is no religious or other group of service workers whose sacrifice and devotion to a cause are greater than the selflessness and loyalty of those who have made weekday church school teaching a career. They have risked much in training themselves for this relatively new calling and have far less vocational and old age security than many religious workers of Protestant and other faiths.

"*If full-time professionally trained teachers are not possible, how can competent teachers be secured?* It is possible to find persons who will do satisfactory work; for example, married women who have been teachers in the public school or directors of religious education, persons who are successful church school workers, retired public school teachers, or social workers with educational training. It is important that all such persons shall have had some acceptable training and experience in religious education." It is possible in many communities to discover a reasonable number of such qualified persons, although with the use of such teachers, who are usually employed on a part-time basis, problems arise —

finding them, holding them on the job (for they have other first interests), deciding upon a rate of pay which is both fair and economical, bringing and keeping their training up-to-date, and the administrative problems consequent upon employing a larger personnel. If a local council has no other alternative, is willing to meet these consequent problems, and is able to employ an unusually competent supervisor, success with a system of this type is possible.

Can we get along with *volunteer teachers?* Yes, if these volunteers meet the same standards of training and experience as those professionally trained, if they make weekday teaching their first love, if they will be regular in meeting their classes, if they will stay on the job as long as the career teachers, and if they have and make regular use of opportunities for in-service training. In actual practice these wishful goals are often maintained with considerable reservations. There are successful weekday systems which have utilized the volunteer plan, sometimes from choice, sometimes from circumstances beyond their control. But in these systems it has been an uphill struggle and their success is due in very large part to an unusually able and heroic director or supervisor. Those who have not been so fortunate in their directors have not fared so well, and are far more likely to be labeled " discontinued."

" *Should ministers teach in these schools?* Ministers, whose qualifications for teaching are equivalent to those of the public school teacher of the grade from which the children come and who are experienced in teaching children of this age, may teach. Practically speaking, most ministers are not accustomed to teaching children, and are more successful with young people. Ministers who undertake this teaching responsibility must see to it that other pastoral and civic duties, however important, do not interfere with regular teaching service." There are doubtless many local situations where ministers can and should be among the teaching staff. But many of them have found that the planning of a lesson is more time-consuming and difficult than preparing a sermon. For the most part, where it has been possible to set up a system using full-time trained teachers, ministers have been its strong backers and have given the weekday system far more than individual teaching service, namely, administrative guidance, and their own and their churches' moral and financial support.

FINDING TEACHERS

How does a local weekday church school system, prospective or established, go about it to find teachers? This, next to queries about courses of study, is a question most frequently asked.

For the system which decides to use part-time paid or volunteer teachers it is obvious that these workers will have to be local persons or persons living fairly near. Names of possible teachers are secured from the ministers, public school leaders, and other sources. A careful screening of the lists of Sunday and vacation church school workers is made, and likewise the lists of those who have taken training courses in community or denominational leadership schools, or both. With these lists in hand, the personnel committee, with the help of the system's supervisor, proceeds with the task of selecting the teachers best qualified.

For the system which will use one or more full-time teachers, it is sometimes possible to discover thoroughly qualified persons within the several groups we mentioned previously. Most frequently, however, it will be necessary to contact outside persons and agencies for suggestions. The personnel committee should write to state council and denominational headquarters. Only a few of these have been able, thus far, to assign major responsibility for weekday work to a staff person, but it is worth an inquiry, since various staff members do come across young people and others who are interested in Christian education careers.

Some of the best sources for prospective teachers are the various colleges, seminaries and schools of Christian education. Increasingly their graduates are looking forward to some kind of religious education career, and this new calling is making an appeal to them. Even in teachers' colleges preparing students for public school teaching, one finds an occasional person who prefers working in the field of religion.

Other persons who can be of assistance in locating teachers are the directors of the larger weekday systems. They may help in two ways. Because of their constant contact with the field and their own endeavors to locate workers, they often have in their files the names of persons, which for one reason or another (preference for a certain section of the country, for example) can be given to some other system. Sometimes a teacher who has had experience in an older system may be secured as a head teacher or supervisor for a new system. This procedure seems only fair to the movement, for it furnishes high-grade direction to a beginning system which it would otherwise lack.

The Department of Weekday Religious Education of the National Council of Churches has been able to render a limited amount of recruitment and placement service for weekday church school teachers and is endeavoring to expand these services. It has furnished colleges and training schools with information and literature intended to enlist

Christian young people in this new calling.[3] It has devised registration, application, and reference forms for gathering and distributing information about prospective workers for local communities. While the number of workers seeking locations is as yet limited and cannot meet the demand, a start is being made. The interest in this new vocation on the part of Christian training schools is most encouraging.

THE WEEKDAY TEACHER'S CONTRIBUTIONS

We began this chapter by calling attention to the high standards for teachers which are set for the weekday church school. Now we would like to point out the unusual opportunity which these teachers have to pioneer in demonstrating new concepts of education. They are challenged to enlarge the boundaries of the teaching programs of the church and of the public school, to both of which the new weekday church school has definite relationships.

In too many instances a weekday church school has been looked upon as a duplicate of the Sunday church school on weekdays. To say that it is much more than that is not to disparage the particular and valuable teaching done by that agency. The weekday church school has contributions all its own, while taking due account of the churches' other Christian education programs and helping to conserve the values of each of them.

In other instances it has been assumed that weekday church school teaching should copy that of the public school. This has been due in large part to the great advances which the latter has made in educational philosophy and teaching methods in the past generation. But, instead of tempering

[3] "A New Career for You — Weekday Religious Education" is the title of a recruiting leaflet which may be secured without charge from the National Council of Churches.

the philosophy and methods of secular education and evolving a concept of Christian teaching inherent in the nature of the Christian religion itself, general education aims and techniques have been too often uncritically applied to religious education. Weekday church school teachers may rightly rejoice in the democratic goals and methods of public education, but they must show in their teaching that democracy owes much to Christianity and that the wonders of science are the handiwork of the Creator and Sustainer of the universe.

As objective after objective, each worthy and commendable, has been adopted and emphasized by the public school the past half century — citizenship training, then character education, and now spiritual values — some church leaders and Christian educators have said: " That's it; it's really what we also are trying to do; we'll make our contribution to it." So often they have failed to see that *Christian* citizenship is more than democratic citizenship; that *Christian* character education is more than teaching an ethical code; that there can be no true teaching of spiritual values if they are not rooted in faith in God.

Thus there comes a challenge to weekday church school teachers, in the unique crossroads religious education program in which they are serving, to demonstrate an improved type of teaching for the churches of the community, and also help the public school teachers discover the ways by which " faith in the Fatherhood of God and the brotherhood of man " can be made the " basis for the life of the school and the personal lives of teachers, students, and citizens in a free and responsible democracy." [4]

[4] *Report of the Committee on Religion and Public Education,* Division of Christian Education, National Council of the Churches of Christ in the U. S. A.

It is to be hoped and expected that weekday church school teachers will play an expanding role in the religious education program of the entire community. There is no reason why, as we have previously indicated, they should not be employed on a year-round basis. In the summer months they can assist the churches in their vacation religious education program — vacation church schools, summer conferences, day camps, and Sunday programs adapted to summer conditions and needs. While the weekday teaching program will require most of their time during the public school year, it should be understood that one of their responsibilities and opportunities is that of acting as " helping teachers " to the volunteer lay workers of the churches, thereby demonstrating that the weekday program is not in competition with the other church teaching agencies, but is a part of the total educational program of the church.

If weekday church school teachers render these leadership training and other services to the local churches, if they work with individual parents and pupils, if they share in the various character building programs for the community, if they co-operate with the public school teachers in ways we have indicated — then they will actually serve as community directors of Christian education, pioneers in service to the ecumenical church.

Collectively weekday church school teachers represent one of the specialized teaching groups in Protestantism. As such, both individually and as a teaching fellowship, they can not only render splendid service to churches and communities, but they will be inspiring examples to questing youth of the satisfaction which comes from a life service dedicated to the Christian cause.

Chapter VI

Administering and Supervising
the Program

HAVING described, in Chapter III, the organization of a local weekday church school system and having emphasized the importance of a strongly based sponsoring agency, we are now ready to suggest how the program should be administered and supervised. Although these two functions are somewhat distinct, and in the larger systems require the services of two or more employed workers, they head up in an administrative board which is the dynamo that keeps the program running smoothly and efficiently.

THE ADMINISTRATIVE BOARD

We have previously mentioned the practical necessity of the larger sponsoring group's having a small executive committee for the purpose of administrative effectiveness.[1] Such a committee in actual working is an administrative board, corresponding to a local public school board. Its membership should be carefully chosen. As in the case of the larger sponsoring group, even though much smaller, it should be as representative as possible of the various persons and groups

[1] See page 36.

concerned with the weekday system. It should include key leaders of the sponsoring agency and other persons added to insure adequate representation. The executive of the church council or its Christian education department should be a member ex-officio.

It goes without saying that this executive committee or board will have a considerable task in getting a new weekday church school program started. It will have to meet frequently, almost continuously for a time. We have recommended at least a year's preparation in launching a solidly built program of weekday religious education for any community. Having stressed the extent and seriousness of the job in getting the program under way, it must also be said that there will not come a time when the work will let up completely. The new system must be kept going. Too often even well-established systems have slumped because the administrative group left the responsibility with one or two members or to the paid director or supervisor.

The administrative activities of the board are many, too many to be listed in detail. In general, subject to action by the sponsoring agency, it will formulate policies and outline the program. It should have authority to transact business between meetings of the sponsoring agency. Its chairman should represent the agency and the board on the inter-faith committee and in meetings with other groups such as the public school authorities, parent-teacher groups, and the like.

Much of the work of the administrative board can be done through special committees, the members of which it will nominate to the sponsoring agency for confirmation at its annual or other meeting. These committee members may be selected from the larger membership of the council and the broad constituency we have described. Five such committees are recommended as a minimum working force—on finance, public relations, publicity and educational promotion, personnel, and curriculum. In smaller communities the work of two or more of these may be given to a single committee. Although the various important aspects of the total weekday church school program, as treated in other chapters in this volume, involve the effective working of these committees, a brief survey of their duties is given here to show the wide scope of activities with which the administrative board is concerned.

DUTIES OF SPECIAL COMMITTEES

The *committee on finance* [2] should take the lead in raising the budget after preparing such a budget to cover salaries and expenses of the staff members, their pensions and other insurance, the cost of curriculum materials and supplies, classroom rental and custodial service, transportation of teachers or pupils, or both, and other items. Naturally, the finance committee will make a complete report of the monies received and expended and will see that there is a regular audit of the weekday system's financial operations.

The *committee on public relations* [3] has a rather extensive task, if it takes its work seriously. It should cultivate the co-operating and potentially co-operating churches both to secure their moral support of the program and to relate it to their other educational agencies. The weekday church school program must be viewed and officially recognized as a part of each church's total religious education program and be so planned and conducted that it thus functions. This com-

[2] See also Chapter VII.
[3] See also Chapter VIII.

mittee has many opportunities to contact and secure the co-operation of the parents of the community. It also has the important responsibility of cultivating friendly relations with the other major faiths and those Protestant groups which may not join in a common teaching program. The relationships of the weekday system to other community agencies, particularly with the public school system and its staff, also fall within the duties of such a committee.

The *committee on publicity and educational promotion* [4] has a great variety of opportunities to interpret the weekday church school. It may use the pulpit, the press, the radio, and television. It should plan for home visitation to secure pupils for the program both from church and non-church homes. It will prepare publicity literature, make use of church bulletins and calendars, exhibits of pupils' work, and speakers in various church and community meetings. Not only is the work of this committee important in launching a new weekday system, it is equally necessary to keep the program continually before the churches and the general public. The successful operation of a local weekday system should not be taken for granted. It needs regular and frequent promotion of an educational character.

The *committee on personnel,* [5] as the name suggests, is responsible for the selection and guidance of staff members — the director, supervisor, and teachers. It will recommend to the sponsoring agency the nature of the contracts, the length of appointment, the salaries and other financial matters which concern employment. It will assist the staff with various problems and see that they are officially recognized and have a welcome place in the church and community life.

[4] See also Chapter IX.
[5] See also Chapter V.

The *committee on curriculum* [6] will take the lead in the planning of the weekday system's program of study, in selecting materials suitable for the courses and relating them to the courses given in the Sunday and vacation church schools and in other units of the churches' educational programs. Membership on this committee requires a specialized type of knowledge and should include persons familiar with public school curricula as well as the needs of the churches, the homes, and the community.

THE SCHOOL ADMINISTRATOR

The administrative board, in the performance of the many functions devolving upon it, will work with and through an employed person, chosen for administrative ability. The title of this person is most frequently that of director of weekday church schools. In most systems the director carries both administrative and supervisory responsibilities. In communities where there are only two or three teachers, one of these often carries the title of head teacher and performs administrative and supervisory duties, as well as teaching.

The weekday church school director clearly has an important job. He or she is chosen on the basis of definite qualifications as noted in *Standards for Weekday Church Schools:* Character — " the kind of Christian personality which attracts others and commands their respect, ability to work with other adults and understand the techniques of counseling in order to bring out the best qualities of those under his guidance "; education — " graduate study in education, administration, the Bible and religious education "; experience — " both in organization and in supervision ";

[6] See also Chapter IV.

continued study — " the habit of continued study and reading in the field for which he gives guidance " and regular attendance at " state and national religious education conferences." [7]

THE DIRECTOR'S DUTIES

What does a weekday church school director do? Instead of attempting a general description of the duties performed by directors, the author has asked two of these busy persons to furnish him with statements of their administrative activities:

Administrative Duties of the Executive Secretary of the Oak Park-River Forest Community Council of Churches. [8]

1. Employment of teachers
     Correspondence, interviews, recommendations

2. Supervision of teaching
     Observation, individual consultation, teachers' meetings

3. Preparation of curriculum
     Planning research, testing, revision
     Consultation with and guidance of committee of Board

4. Scheduling of classes
     Contact with school authorities, conference with school schedule committee
     Locating classrooms in churches and nearby buildings

5. Transportation necessities
     Police protection at crossings
     Bus requirements, scheduling

[7] See page 7 of booklet.
[8] Daniel R. Ehalt.

6. Promotion of enrollment
    Church representatives in local churches
    School class lists through P.-T.A.
    Phone callers for class lists
    Mailing of announcements and permit cards

7. Commencement
    Graduation papers by eighth graders
    Selection of best papers and five student speakers
    Diplomas presented by officers of Board
    Participation in service by several ministers
    Music by units from public schools

8. Records
    Class rolls
    Attendance reports to office
    Report cards to parents
    Permanent record of class work by semesters

9. Annual meeting
    Delegate lists from pastors
    Invitations to delegates
    Programs planned with assistance of a committee
      of the Board

10. Publicity
    Brochures
    Newsletters
    Annual Reports
    Newspaper articles

11. Meeting financial requirements
    Church budget appropriations
    Tuition for weekday classes
    Individual contributions — mail campaign and
      personal solicitations
    Consultation with and assistance of committee of
      Board

Duties and Relationships of the Weekday Church School Director of the Church Federation of Greater Dayton.[9]

Major Duties

Organization, administration, and supervision of all Weekday Church School classes in the city and county annually including:

Personnel — Supervision

Preparation of the staff for the task (planning conference in September and evaluation conference in June)

Locating good prospects for the department (following through with application blanks, reference forms, interviews, etc.)

Preparing new staff members for work in this community

Guidance of regular weekly staff meetings and called study and work meetings of the staff

Selecting, training, and preparing all class substitutes

Serving as a Weekday Church School teacher part time (a director-teacher)

Supervising all Weekday Church School classes and representing the department in all important class projects

Organization and Administration

Schedule making with the public schools and pupil registration

Organizing and administering all community contracts for Weekday Church School work (with added responsibility of raising all contract funds and caring for transportation schedules and monthly accounts)

Responsibility for all relationship with the P.-T.A.'s of the city and county and their annual contributions to the Church Federation Campaign

Guidance of Weekday Church School Committee and its sub-committees; and its coordinating council project

Plans with church boards for church centers for Weekday Church School classes

[9] Florence Martin.

Guidance of office assistance needed by the department (preparing a yearly, monthly, and weekly work schedule)

Preparation of all department promotional and publicity materials in connection with Publicity Committee of Weekday Church School Committee

Guiding all staff home visitation

Gathering monthly staff reports (on community contacts and program statistics)

Preparing statistical reports for public school principals and superintendents (the first month and each semester)

Preparation of all department mimeographing

Preparation of all copy for correspondence and reports

Preparing and conducting special programs in the public schools, churches and P.-T.A. groups especially at Christmastime and Christian Church Festival season

Preparation of needed curricular and other materials for the department

Gathering and keeping accumulative records of children

Advising and guiding those who look to the Dayton Weekday Church Schools for enlightenment

Minor Responsibilities

Care of Weekday Church School department staff library and department files

Ordering, storing, and distributing all equipment and supplies needed by the school classes

Annual inventory of stock in the office and schools (seeking staff school requisitions annually)

Guidance of the repair of the equipment

Preparation of church janitors for the task

Preparation of church service accounts each semester

Preparation of bus fare accounts monthly

Preparation of staff expense accounts each two weeks

Preparation of substitute bills regularly

Caring for Weekday Church School offerings to worthy causes

Making available "Thoughts of God" and other Christian literature for sale to students

Guiding the staff in preparation of Family Booklets as guidance of family life at Church Festival times, Family Week, etc.

Acting as booklet editor

In the weekday church school systems in smaller communities, of which there are many, there is usually only one teacher, who is administrator, self-supervisor, and teacher all in one. In these situations, a considerable share of the administrative work must devolve upon the administrative board and its chairman. It therefore behooves the board members to be well informed and on the job to see that everything goes as it should.

EDUCATIONAL SUPERVISION

The function of supervision in a weekday church school system is somewhat distinct from that of administration although it is usually one of the duties of the director or other administrator, as will be seen from the foregoing lists. A descriptive definition of supervision, as given by Frank M. McKibben, one of the pioneer leaders in the weekday movement, sets forth its particular purposes as follows:

1. To guide those responsible for Christian education in studying the total program as it is being provided in the light of the most representative standards of their denomination and of Protestantism in general;
2. To lead workers into a fuller understanding of the nature and meaning of Christian nurture and of the conditions necessary for its fullest realization;
3. To aid workers in the various aspects of the program to determine the objectives they may seek in their work and to help them discover the extent to which they are being achieved;

4. To develop among teachers and leaders a willingness and ability to analyze and objectively to evaluate the procedures and materials they are using with a view to determining the elements of strength and weakness and to undertake specific measures of improvement;

5. To develop schedules and measuring instruments by which the program may be more accurately evaluated and to train workers in their use;

6. To carry forward continuously a program of enlistment, motivation, training, and placement in service of men and women who will be needed to carry forward the total program;

7. To help educate the parents and total constituency of the church in the necessity and importance of Christian education and to encourage and provide for their active participation in and support of the program.[10]

Those who organize and conduct a weekday church school must clearly recognize and provide for supervision. Unless the educational quality of the program maintains a high level, no matter how well the system is organized and supported, it will go down hill and quite likely become a " noble experiment " that failed. To repeat: it is our honest conviction, and that of weekday church school advocates generally, that the major problem of the movement is that of high standards. This makes good supervision an indispensable factor in a weekday church school system, large or small.

In what has been described as a period of " mushroom growth," it has been natural that this indigenous type of religious education program should have sprouted " here, there and everywhere." Many of the local programs have developed and grown quite without relationship to any

[10] *Guiding Workers in Christian Education* (Abingdon Press), p. 12.

supervisory agency. This is one reason for program failures, for too many communities have proceeded without consideration of a wrong way or a right way. It is to be hoped that the further development of this growing movement will see these isolated local weekday schools brought together into supervisory districts and receive the benefits of " wise direction and careful guidance," to use a phrase from a policy statement of the National Council of Churches. One method of doing this and affording a high quality of educational supervision is the " contract plan." In areas where there is a well-organized weekday church school system covering a large city, smaller communities nearby have asked for a part of the time of the city system's teachers, say one day a week. With this teacher's time goes also the services of the city system's efficient director, so that the pupils in the smaller community are assured of just as fine teaching as their " city cousins."

The person who is to be responsible for supervision should have a superior type of Christian personality and be able to work with people, both young and old. He or she should be a college graduate and have had graduate study with a specialty in supervision as well as in Bible and religious education; should have had successful experience in teaching either in the public school or in a weekday church school and, desirably, experience in supervision in either or both of these types of school; and should continue in study and attend state and national religious education conferences.

One of the most important of these conferences is the annual meeting of the Weekday Religious Education Section of the National Council of Churches. Membership in and regular attendance at its meetings is practically a must for every weekday church school director and supervisor. Local systems should make it possible for their teachers also to become members of this national weekday workers group and attend its meetings on a rotating schedule if not every year.

A "HELPING TEACHER"

Prerequisite to and more important than the use of any particular method of supervision is the attitude which both the weekday church school supervisor and the teachers hold with regard to their mutual relationships and the manner in which supervisory activities are conducted. Real, effective supervision is not " snooper-vision " (spying). Nor is it to be carried on in an atmosphere of superiority-inferiority (hunting for mistakes instead of being constructively critical). Nor is it merely " casting a genial influence " (praising but giving no real help). The relationship which is most fruitful is that in which the supervisor plays the role of consultant or " helping teacher." These titles suggest that one teacher, with more experience and more training, shares her knowledge in a friendly and democratic manner with one who is searching for this very help.

WAYS OF SUPERVISION

The methods which may be used by a weekday church school supervisor to improve the quality of teaching in her system are many. We can mention only a few, and refer inquiring supervisors to more detailed sources of help.

One of the best and most generally employed methods of assisting teachers to do better is to observe them at work. How to do this is suggested by the following quotation made with adaptations from an earlier volume by the author:[11]

[11] Shaver, Erwin L., *Shall Laymen Teach Religion?* (New York: Richard R. Smith), pp. 123-24.

Before visiting a weekday church school class, the observing supervisor should make preparation. She should frame a simple set of questions and directions for her visit which she may keep in mind as she watches what goes on. It is quite essential also that she look forward to and carry through her visit in the spirit of sympathetic co-operation with the teacher whose teaching she is observing.

She should note, as she visits, such items as: (1) the general situation in which the teaching is being carried on; (2) what happens as the class proceeds; (3) the significant events; (4) the desirable and undesirable happenings; and (5) the experiences which seem to have particular value for the future program of the weekday church school as a whole.

The following are questions which will help the supervisor to measure the educational effectiveness of the class session:

1. Were the pupils active and interested?
2. Was the activity directed and purposeful?
3. Did it include every individual?
4. Was there thinking going on?
5. Was there growth of life and purpose?
6. Was there a Christian motive for the activity?
7. Was there a consciousness of fulfilling Christ's purpose?
8. Was there an attitude of worship?
9. Did the activity lead on to further activity, such as a service of worship, a program of recreation, a service project or a plan for study and investigation?

Another commonly used procedure is individual conference with the teacher to be helped. Sometimes it will be based upon an observation of teaching; at other times it will be occasioned by some particular situation which has arisen; at still other times it will be routine, but nevertheless friendly and constructive. It is not always necessary to have conferences on an individual teacher basis. Sometimes several teachers with the same problem or need can be met in a group conference.

Coaching in the use of curriculum materials is a most effective method of teacher improvement. This is a method whereby teachers, individually or in groups, are helped lesson by lesson or unit by unit to plan and teach their courses. It is especially helpful to beginning teachers. It is one of the best leadership training methods, for it is " on the job " and gives immediate help and confidence to the teacher. It also furnishes the supervisor with an understanding of the particular needs of the teacher and enables her to give just the kind of guidance and help that the teacher needs, but which might not otherwise be apparent.[12]

In a number of weekday systems using part-time and volunteer teachers it has been considered very necessary to conduct regular teacher training courses with the understanding that all teachers should take them. This goal has not always been attained, but where it has, the quality of teaching has been definitely improved.

Observation and laboratory schools are increasing in number and deserved popularity, for they are very effective as methods of improving teaching skill. Wise is that weekday system which regularly sends its workers to these schools.

There are also a number of informal methods of teacher training and improvement which have been employed by supervisors according to their local needs and interests. Among these are regular and special bulletins sent to the teachers containing practical and inspirational materials; the use of rating forms, score cards, inventories, goal cards,

[12] See the pamphlet, *Coaching Your Teachers,* National Council of Churches.

and the like; true-false and other types of test to bring forth problems and needs; teacher problem sheets; the making and keeping of a weekday church school teacher's notebook (containing inspirational materials, individual pupil records, classified resources, lesson plans, and so forth); suggestions for special reading and study; furnishing the teachers with subscriptions to religious education journals. All these and others of similar character stimulate teacher growth.

In the best weekday church school systems supervisors and teachers share in curriculum construction and reconstruction. To them the curriculum is a living and growing experience for which the printed materials are but the guide. In this type of co-operative project all have a sense of comradeship and personal achievement, and teacher enrichment is assured.

The good supervisor also seeks in various ways to keep her teachers encouraged and inspired. Sometimes this is done by deserved face-to-face commendation, sometimes by writing a personal note, sometimes by furnishing them with inspirational materials. These attentions and appreciations pay off in many ways.

In closing our chapter it cannot be too strongly emphasized that the relation of the weekday church school administrator — director or supervisor or both—to the teaching staff must accord with the best educational procedures and the democratic spirit. The total staff must work as a group. Each one should be encouraged and helped to share in setting goals, making and executing plans, and evaluating results. Blessed are the weekday church school administrators, supervisors, and teachers who exemplify in their mutual relationships the principles of Christian living which they would teach to their children.

Chapter VII

Financing the Program

YEARS AGO, when the author surveyed the weekday religious education movement for the Religious Education Association, he received among the replies to his questionnaire this response: " We are glad to report that our weekday church school last year cost us just three cents per pupil! " Without passing judgment upon the quality of work done in this particular school, many contacts with weekday church schools through the years warrant the assertion that successful and permanent schools cannot be supported on this penny-pinching basis. In the light of increasingly accepted standards for both public education and religious education generally and the claims for the unique quality of work done by this type of church school, a new level of expenditure must be envisioned.

Therefore, among the committees recommended for appointment by the sponsoring agency is a committee on finance consisting of at least three persons selected for their particular talents in this respect. This committee has two primary responsibilities: first, making up a recommended budget of expenditures, and second, taking the lead in devising and carrying through plans for raising the adopted budget. Its task will be much the same whether this budget is a part of a larger budget for all co-operative church work in the community or an independent budget specifically for the weekday church school system. In both situations there is the necessity for considerable and painstaking work on the part of the committee. It should go without saying that, as the *Standards* indicate, " full reports should be made of all receipts and expenditures and all books and vouchers should be audited carefully." [1]

MAKING UP THE BUDGET

Many of the same items are included in the budgets of most weekday church school systems, whether they are large or small, even though the amounts to be expended will vary with the size of the system. The important thing is that the finance committee recognize the necessity of caring for these several items as required costs for a high quality program.

First among these costs are the salaries of the employed staff — director, or supervisor and teachers, or both — which " whether on full or part time, should follow the scale of the public schools." In addition to salaries there should be a budget item to care for these workers' retirement or annuity pensions. A number of weekday systems have some form of pension system; some are enrolled in the national social security program. Insurance covering accident, health, and hospitalization is also becoming standard procedure for religious organizations and is included in the budgets of many weekday systems. There are various expenses connected with the work of staff members which should be provided by the sponsoring agency — office rental, secretarial help, travel expense from one teaching center to another whether by public transportation or by automobile, incidental postage and telephone charges, and provision for expenses in attending professional gatherings such as we have previously mentioned. All of these provisions add to the efficiency of the workers. To expect these not-too-well-paid

[1] *Standards for Weekday Church Schools,* p. 9.

servants of the church and community to pay for them out of their salaries is hardly fair.

Another important item in a well-planned budget is the charge in connection with the housing of classes — a reasonable rental charge, whether the classes meet in churches or in other places, to cover heating, lighting, custodial service, and the like. Experience has shown that it is best to have a definite arrangement in this matter, even in the case of church buildings. There are housing expenses where homes are used as classrooms — extra folding chairs, a special covering for the floor, light, heat, and so forth. When mobile classrooms are employed to meet the needs of areas where there are no conveniently located churches, there are, obviously, operating expenses, aside from the original cost, which must be considered.

An expenditure item of central importance is provision for curriculum materials. We have already indicated that the early (and some later!) weekday systems have tried to skimp at this point by providing rather sketchy outlines for the teacher and often nothing for the pupil. As standards have risen, much better curriculum materials have been developed. The cost of these is not large, certainly not when compared with the price of public school texts, which must be paid for even though out of school taxes! Most of the Co-operative Texts provide a teacher's guide for the year's course for two dollars or less; the average cost of pupil's books is thirty-five cents a semester. Other good course materials are about the same price. It has sometimes been the practice to ask the parents to pay for the children's books. This works satisfactorily in communities where the family economic level is fairly high and uniform. But it makes for considerable embarrassment and extra work for the teacher to see that some of the less fortunate children are cared for, particularly those having no previous church connection. For these the weekday church school has a special responsibility and the opportunity of enrolling them should not be jeopardized by expecting payment for texts. Generally the better plan is to include this item in the budget.

In addition to these, there are many items of equipment (chairs, tables, audio-visual aids, musical instruments, and so forth); Bibles, hymnals and other religious education books; and the usual run of tools (paper, pencils, chalk, paste, and so on). Overlooking budget provisions for these teaching materials either puts the burden on the teacher or some benevolent friend, or the quality of teaching suffers from their lack or scarcity.

In a well-thought-out budget there are other items of expenditure needed to make the system run well. One of these is an amount to care for publicity, although some of this can be secured without special expenditure. The several committees also have expenses in carrying on their work and an amount for each should be included in the total budget.

In keeping with our rather detailed mention of these many budget items, it is suggested that the budget committee make use of *Standards for Weekday Church Schools* as a check list to see that no important item be omitted.

SAMPLE BUDGETS

To make concrete the various types of expenditure required in running an efficient weekday church school system, the budgets of two successful weekday systems are given below. The first is that of a large city system; the second that of a county system, operating in a dozen small towns and rural townships.

Weekday Church School Budget of the
Council of Churches of Greater Cincinnati [2]

Note: This budget represents the direct expenditure of the Council of Churches. Most of the schools are financed by the local communities, whose combined budgets amount to about forty thousand dollars.

Rent		$ 744
Telephone		300
Salaries		
Director	$4,260	
Secretary	3,540	7,800
Director's Expense		500
Social Security		158
Retirement Insurance		550
General Promotion *		200
Conference Expense —		
Director and Teachers		550
Teachers' Salaries †		6,100
Transportation —		
Condon School ‡		400
Social Security		140
Printing §		200
Supplies		300
Heat and Light —		
Ellen House ¶		200
Sick Leave		65
Curriculum		50
National Council of		
Churches		13
Total		$18,270

* Such as printing of descriptive folder.
† The budget of the Council includes financing of some schools in underprivileged areas and special schools.
‡ This is a school for crippled children.
§ Parents' request cards and record sheets.
¶ Ellen House is used to house weekday classes in a neighborhood where there is no church available.

[2] Elizabeth M. Hanna, Director of Religious Education.

Weekday Church School Budget of the Morgan County, Indiana, Schools of Weekday Religious Education [3]

Salary and Travel Expense, Two Teachers	$ 6,180
Curriculum and Materials	500
Room Rental and Transportation	2,052
Commencement, Insurance and Bonds, Equipment, Supplies, and Miscellaneous	1,268
Total	$10,000

Note: The churches support the program on the basis of two dollars per active member. Many individuals, Bible schools, and civic organizations also contribute.

RAISING THE BUDGET

Having made up a budget of the financial needs of the weekday church school program, the committee on finance must next face the harder task of raising it, or assisting in raising the total budget of the sponsoring agency, if that agency is a council of churches or council of Christian education. One of the questions frequently asked in conferences is: " How is the money raised for a weekday church school program? " Therefore, the following suggestions as to how it is done.

The most common and probably the best method is to have each co-operating church in the community accept a quota representing its share of the total. There are various methods of arriving at a fair share for each church. One is to devise a formula, which may be based upon several factors — the membership of each church, the number of pupils in its Sunday church school, and the financial ability of the church as shown by its annual current expense budget. The author is of the opinion that the latter basis is the most fair,

[3]Alvin J. Whitaker, Chairman of the Executive Board.

although some finance committees prefer to take into account all three and other factors also. It should be said here that the practice, followed in some communities, of setting the quota on the sole basis of the number of children from each church enrolled or to be enrolled in the weekday program is an unsatisfactory one. It does not take into consideration the large number of un-churched children who attend the classes, whereas one of the primary objectives of the weekday program is to reach these un-churched boys and girls who most need the teaching. Whatever the formula employed, the quota when accepted is usually added to the local churches' annual budgets, which insures prompt payment in most cases.

A second and frequent method of raising the budget is to have an annual community-wide campaign, in which churches, individuals, service clubs and lodges, community industries, and other agencies are solicited for gifts. When carefully planned and conducted these campaigns are usually successful. They have the special merit of informing the community about the program and having a large number of people feel that they have a stake in it. One drawback is the multiplicity of local drives with which such a campaign has to compete.

Quite often the question is raised as to whether it is possible to secure help from community chests. The answer is generally a negative one, although a few cases have been reported in which help has been given. The author recalls one instance where such help, representing a considerable portion of the weekday budget, had been coming from the chest, but was to be shortly withdrawn, much to the consternation of those who had depended, too assuredly, upon it.

Whether there is a timed local drive for the weekday

budget or not, one source of support is individuals who are willing and able to make special gifts. Sometimes these contributors are not individuals but foundations. Naturally such gifts are most welcome, unless they have compromising strings attached to them. The problem is that of depending too much upon the gifts of such persons or agencies, for, if and when they are withdrawn, the budget shrinkage must be cared for, lest the program be cut down or have to stop entirely.

In a few situations a plan of charging tuition is used to help finance weekday church schools. This practice is of doubtful value, except in communities with a high economic level, with family incomes evenly distributed. It usually requires a system of supplementary scholarships to care for those who cannot or do not pay up.

Another practice is that of taking a special offering from the parents and pupils. This is not to be depended upon to care for any large part of the budget, but may be a helpful supplement.

Various other means have been used to raise money for the program — sales, fairs, dramatic and musical performances, offerings at graduation exercises, and the like. These too should not be primary means of budget raising, but have supplementary value.

A final word of advice: It is definitely illegal to use public funds for a weekday religious education program of the type we are discussing in this volume. The author has come across several instances where this practice, directly or indirectly, has been followed. In more than one instance one hour a week of the public school teacher's time, during the regular school hours for which she was employed and paid, was being given to teaching weekday religious education classes. In one community the public school principal took it upon herself in her official capacity and while in the public school to collect the cost of the weekday church school pupils' texts. Any such financial aid is clearly unconstitutional.

AS MUCH FOR RELIGIOUS EDUCATION

Standards for Weekday Church Schools advises: "As much money should be spent for religious education courses as for other school subjects in proportion to the time given to them." A study of local public school costs per pupil will " help in determining what is a reasonable expenditure for a weekday church school in your area." According to a research bulletin issued by the National Education Association, the figures given for the various states ranged from $85 to $324 per pupil per year, with an average for the entire United States of $217 per pupil.[4] These costs are increasing steadily.

Our Protestant citizens, both parents who have children to send to our public schools, and those who are not parents, willingly pay taxes for these schools and are justly proud of them. They believe they are getting their money's worth in terms of cultural knowledge, vocational skill, citizenship training, and character development for the boys and girls of America. But these same citizens are not yet fully aware of their grossly inadequate contribution to the definite teaching of religion as compared to that given for secular education. It ill behooves those whose spiritual ancestors laid the foundations of the public school system and put religion at the heart of the curriculum, to have gradually neglected, in financial support, the most important subject

[4] *Educational Differences Among the States,* 1954.

in the child's course of study. The weekday church school will succeed only in proportion to its success in meeting the standards held for education as a whole and acceptance of the financial responsibility involved.

What does this mean in terms of the amount to be spent per pupil per year? Usually the weekday church school classes meet one hour a week, which represents one twenty-fifth of the time given to general education subjects. Dividing the annual expenditure per pupil for public education by twenty-four gives about nine dollars as a fair measure of expenditure for an hour a week of religious instruction. Obviously in some states this would be high in comparison with public school instruction costs; in others considerably lower, depending upon the extent to which the particular state expenditure falls below or exceeds the national average.

There are various other factors which affect the annual cost per pupil figure. When the weekday church school class enrollment is considerably smaller than that of the public school grade, the per pupil cost may run higher. When a system of pupil transportation is necessary the cost is increased. When the teachers are paid an inadequate salary, the cost may be lowered, but at the considerable sacrifice of those who have chosen to be teachers of religion rather than other subjects.

WILL OUR CHURCHES BE OUT-TAUGHT?

Let us turn from a comparison of the costs of teaching religion with those for secular education and look at the amounts which other religious groups are spending for their various programs for including religion in the child's daily education.

A statement received from the Department of Education

of the National Catholic Welfare Conference, as to the annual expenditure per pupil for Roman Catholic parochial schools, says: " The average expenditure per pupil would be between $72 and $84." This relatively low figure is made possible by the fact that the sisters who teach in these parochial schools receive only " $50 to $60 a month and their shelter." [5]

The staff member in charge of schools for the Lutheran Church, Missouri Synod, Board of Parish Education[6] states: " Judging from a survey I made . . . the cost per child in our (parochial) schools runs from $175 to $250 per year, per capita." This figure must be viewed in the light of the fact that these parochial schools use trained teachers who are paid at a rate essentially equal to the salaries of public school teachers.

A report received from the Department of Education of the Church of Jesus Christ of Latter Day Saints regarding the expenditure of this religious group for its " seminary " (high school) program of weekday religious education previously referred to, shows an average of over $32 per pupil annually. The teachers in this weekday religious education program meet the accepted standards for public school teachers in the states where the program is being conducted and are paid at a comparable rate.

Many Jewish groups conduct an after-school and evening program of religious education. According to a bulletin issued by the United Synagogue Commission on Jewish Education, " The Objectives and Standards for the Congregational School," " Experience has shown that the cost of in-

[5] Sister Mary Josetta, in an address at the Chicago meeting of the National Catholic Education Association, 1954.

[6] The Rev. A. C. Stellhorn.

struction, exclusive of heat, light, secretarial service and other overhead expenses, in a weekday school offering six hours of instruction per week and having an enrollment of 150 pupils is approximately $70 per child per year."

A detailed study of local church programs of Christian education, made by a typical Protestant denomination, the Presbyterian Church in the United States, has revealed an average annual expenditure for Christian teaching of $3.96 per pupil. This study, made under the leadership of an outstanding religious educator, summarizes the critical situation in these sentences: " In the modern world there are five contenders for supremacy in man's inner world, and thus finally for the shaping of his outer world as well — fascism, communism, secular democracy, Roman Catholicism, and Protestantism. *And of these five, the first four wage an aggressive education program with vast resources at command and with the highest skill, while Protestantism plays at the fringes of the game with tepid devotion."* [7]

IF OTHERS CAN . . .

If other religious groups can raise the funds to support a strong religious education program, there is no reason why our Protestant churches should not be able to do likewise. Certainly we are not to be excused on the basis that we represent a lower income group! In fact, there are a number of low income religious groups of Protestant persuasion, not usually affiliated with our councils of churches, whose proportionate giving for Christian education far exceeds the rest of us.

The author is convinced that a new level of Christian edu-

[7] *Lift Up Your Eyes,* Lewis J. Sherrill (Richmond : John Knox Press), p. 155.

cation expenditure is possible, not only for weekday church schools but for other church educational agencies as well. The very fact that hundreds of local communities have enthusiastically adopted and put into operation an adequately financed weekday system is clear evidence that others can do likewise. The choice between a well-financed system and one which costs little or nothing seems to be a matter of geography or of personal persuading rather than considered judgment based upon a careful, nation-wide study of weekday church school patterns. There are large areas in the country where nothing less than a schedule of staggered excusal of pupils, the use of full-time trained teachers, and other educationally desirable practices mark the program. Elsewhere, there are other areas where the patterns include practices which work against educational standards because " money just couldn't be raised " for this type of Christian education. It is largely a matter of a point of view, which we hope will become one which is more and more committed to strong financial support for the program.

This hope seems to be increasingly justified. The consecrated teachers making weekday religious education their Christian vocation are winning their way in the communities where they work. As state and local councils of churches have become stronger they have raised their standards for this as well as for other types of program activities. They have also discovered that a financially well-supported weekday program is a powerful " selling point " in raising their total budgets. It should also be mentioned that public school leaders favor well-supported and educationally high level weekday church school programs for their communities, both because they themselves are trained persons and because they therefore know that the period of excusal has been profitably spent. The national denominational boards of Christian education, as they have watched the expansion and strengthening of this new program, are sure that the successful type of weekday church school is one that has a firm financial undergirding.

Chapter VIII

Relations With Community Agencies

WHEN the weekday church school movement was in its infancy, the superintendent of public instruction of a western state raised this question: " Who is responsible for these weekday church school classes — the public schools or the churches?" In those earlier years the answer to such a question was somewhat uncertain, since it was assumed by some that weekday religious education classes were an integral part of the public school system. In later years both practical and legal considerations have strengthened the view that weekday church schools such as we are describing are the responsibility of the individual churches or inter-church organization to whose custody the parents have asked that their children be transferred for religious instruction.

The acceptance of this point of view, however, does not mean that other community agencies are not concerned. In its effective operation the weekday church school is a crossroads school representing the common concerns of the home, the church, and the public school with respect to religious instruction in the child's total educational program. Unless the parents and the public school authorities as well as the churches co-operate heartily and actively, the work of the weekday church school is greatly hampered. It is the purpose of this chapter to indicate the relationships which this school should maintain with these three and other community agencies.

In the light of these agency concerns it is exceedingly important to have a live committee on public relations. As set forth in the *Standards*, " this committee should be charged with establishing and continually improving the relations of the weekday church school with various community agencies." [1] Some weekday systems do not have such a committee and operate in the blind faith that these relationships will take care of themselves, which they do not. As we proceed we shall point out a number of specific relationships which the committee should establish and improve.

A PARENTS' SCHOOL

As previously indicated, the weekday church school legally rests upon the rights of parents to have religion included within the hours allotted to their children's education. In fulfillment of this intention they request the churches to set up a complementary type school for this purpose, since religion cannot legally be taught by the public school. Said the Supreme Court in its decision in the Zorach case: " Government may not finance religious groups nor undertake religious instruction nor blend secular and sectarian education nor use secular institutions to force one or some religion on any person." [2]

[1] See page 10 of booklet.
[2] Just what can and should be done with reference to religion by the public schools is now the subject of considerable discussion. Two significant reports of recommended policy and procedure are : *Moral and Spiritual Values in the Public Schools*, by the Educational Policies Commission of the National Education Association, and *The Function of the Public Schools in Dealing with Religion*, by the Committee on Education of the American Council on Education.

It is therefore necessary that one of the parents of every child enrolled in a weekday church school program conducted on school time should present a signed request for his excusal. The usual practice is for the sponsoring agency to have such a request card printed in duplicate.[3] One portion is addressed to the public school asking for the excusal of the child from the school at such an hour or hours as have been arranged for his religious instruction. The other portion is addressed to the sponsoring agency indicating the parent's desire that the child be enrolled in the weekday class suitable for his age and public school progress. Both portions are to be signed. One of them becomes the registration roll of the weekday church school system, and its receipt and acceptance makes this agency legally and otherwise responsible for the child while under its jurisdiction. It is for this reason that many weekday systems carry insurance against possible accidents to children. Occasionally, as we have explained in Chapter III, it becomes necessary for the sponsoring agency to refuse continuance of instruction for the child because of repeated unexcused absence, unco-operative behavior or lack of instructional facilities. In such cases the system asks the parent to withdraw his request for his child's excusal. Problem children, however, should be denied the privileges of the weekday church school only after there has been consultation with the guidance agencies of the public school and the community.

It should be said that the underlying philosophy of this type of school is that it is not a substitute for home instruction in religion, although it may be the only religious teaching which the child is receiving when he first enrolls in the

[3] See also page 39.

weekday school. Friends of the weekday program are as concerned, as all persons interested in the religious education of children are, that the home should be the primary school of religion. Therefore, they have faith that, having begun to teach the child whose parents have heretofore been indifferent to his home religious training, these parents will become interested and will both assume their home training responsibilities and co-operate with the church in its various programs for children. Where this faith has been implemented with practical procedures for co-operation with the homes, the results have been most encouraging. It is one of the stars in the crown of the weekday church school that it has been a most effective evangelistic and missionary agency.

LINKS WITH THE HOME

In maintaining effective relations with the homes of its pupils there are several practical methods of contact and service. One of the most important, both for doing better teaching in the weekday classes and for assisting parents, is home visitation by the weekday teachers. Such visits give the weekday teacher a better understanding of the family's religious background and the particular needs of the child and furnish an opportunity to share with the parents the basic aims of the weekday church school teaching. The better weekday systems make definite provision in the work schedules of their teachers for visitation as well as for class teaching. While at least one visit a year in the home of each pupil is a worthy goal for a weekday teacher, visits in the homes of problem children are a must. Those weekday systems where this has become standard procedure have been most heartened by the responses on the part of both parents and children. Countless human interest stories could be told of such enrichment experiences which are a significant part of the weekday teaching program.

Another link connecting the weekday church school with the home is the parent-teacher association. Contrary to some popular impressions these organizations are not public but private in character. They are therefore free, as the public school is not, to use their machinery in behalf of religious teaching in general and the weekday church school program in particular. While practical policy and fair-mindedness wisely prevent these parents' groups from favoring one religion over another, they are not kept from giving whatever help they can to any and all worthy efforts in behalf of the community's children. Consequently, these agencies can be of definite assistance to the local weekday religious education programs. They often help in discovering and registering pupils, or furnishing lists of school children to the weekday church school system. At their meetings the weekday cause and its needs and opportunities may be presented for consideration and positive action.

Wise indeed are those weekday church school systems which keep the parents informed about the program in general and the progress of the individual pupils. The values of regular and frequent contacts by mail or by the pupils themselves, or both, are obvious — information which the parent should have, stimulation of parental interest, suggestions as to how parents may share in the program and the like. To fail to make use of these contacts is missing a great opportunity to strengthen the program.

Since linking the home and the weekday church school involves a two-way relationship, practical methods of helping parents in their home teaching of religion is as important as methods of getting the parents to assist the weekday school. Some weekday systems furnish parents with helpful religious education materials for home use, particularly at special seasons — Christmas, Easter, Thanksgiving, and other church and national festivals.

A SCHOOL OF THE CHURCHES

Historically, we recall that weekday church schools sprang from a local community interest in establishing a new and somewhat independent type of religious education agency. While it then had and still has increasingly strong grass roots support, it has been somewhat of an orphan so far as the individual churches are concerned. But as time has passed, and now that the legality of the new agency has been confirmed, there has come a challenge to the churches to adopt the orphan.[4]

The weekday church school should be in every sense a school *of* the church, *by* the church, and *for* the church. It is one unit in the total educational program of the churches, with the unique characteristics we have previously noted, but essentially a church program. Its success depends in the final analysis upon whether it is supported, both morally and financially, by the churches. It has many contributions to make to the churches' life and teaching, including improved instruction, reaching un-churched children, effective inter-church co-operation, and expansion of their teaching programs.

It is for these reasons that the committee on public relations is urged to work with the local churches to bring

[4] See the statement by denominational educational leaders at the conclusion of this volume.

about this adoption to the extent that it has not yet taken place. "The weekday church school should be officially recognized as a part of the total program of religious education in the participating churches" states the *Standards*.[5] To make this recognition more than a formal vote or a taken-for-granted affair, we find explicit directions given in the National Council of Churches manual, *The Board of Christian Education in the Local Church,* in answer to the question, "What is the (local church) board's responsibility for the weekday church school?"

> **CO-OPERATION.** Co-operate with other churches of the community in making plans for a Protestant interchurch system of weekday church schools. Only when there is no other with which any co-operation is possible would a church be justified in attempting its own weekday church school on released time.

> **EDUCATE AND INFORM.** Seek to educate the membership of the local church and its leaders as to the values of weekday religious education in the community and the procedures for setting up the program.

> **COMMUNITY ORGANIZATION.** Help in setting up a community organization to sponsor and direct a program of weekday religious education, in interpreting the values, standards, and procedures to public school leaders, parents, and citizens generally, and in seeking moral and financial support for it.

> **PROGRAM.** Co-operate with the community organization such as a council of churches in determining when and how the program shall be organized, the areas and grades in which the program shall be set up, the places for holding the classes, the super-

[5] See page 10 of booklet.

vision, and teaching staff and all other administrative details.

ATTENDANCE. Plan for securing attendance of as many pupils as possible from the church school and seek correlation between the weekday church school, and the other educational programs of the church and community.

REPORTS. Arrange for adequate reports to the church as to the progress of the weekday church school and the local church's participation in it and make recommendations on how to improve the participation.[6]

The working relationship between the community weekday church school system and the local churches will become more and more effective as the movement progresses and the directions given above are implemented by the combined efforts of the local church boards of Christian education and the committee on public relations of the weekday system. Two directions of effort are recommended in the *Standards* for the latter committee:

"As far as possible, the program and curriculum of these churches should be considered in setting up the program and curriculum of the weekday church school system.

"Weekday church school teachers should develop a working relation with Sunday church school teachers teaching the same age group which they are teaching in the weekday classes. This will assist them in correlating the weekday program more closely with that conducted by the churches on Sunday."[7]

The first of these counsels has received consideration in Chapter IV and the second in Chapter V. A zealous com-

[6] See page 10 of manual.
[7] See page 10 of booklet.

mittee on public relations will find a real task, but a rewarding opportunity, in working with the committees on personnel and curriculum to carry them out.

RECRUITS FOR THE CHURCH

We mentioned previously that one of the contributions which a weekday church school program makes to the church is the recruiting of un-churched children and their families. How this is done in a well-administered weekday system is shown in these excerpts of a descriptive article:[8]

There are several steps in this recruiting plan. First, the weekday teachers make a survey of unchurched pupils each year and prepare a list for future use. The information is secured from the enrollment cards in the office. Each card contains the Parents' Request Blank for the pupils to be enrolled in the weekday class. The enrollment blank on the reverse gives full information as to church attendance. During the year 1375 unchurched children, with their addresses and fathers' names, were listed as a basis for this work.

A form letter is sent to several ministers in the area in which the school is conducted. The letter is worth quoting as it tells its own story briefly:

"You will find enclosed a list of unchurched pupils (those who report they do not attend a Sunday school). A similar list is being sent to other ministers in the school district. They are attending weekday church school at (name of church in which classes are held). We are very anxious to get these children to attend Sunday church school regularly.

"We would greatly appreciate any assistance you can give us in helping these children to become members of Sunday church schools. We would be glad to know

[8] Rest, Friedrich, "Weekday Schools Recruit for Sunday Schools," *International Journal of Religious Education.*

what use is made of this list and which children do start in your Sunday church school.

" This list of unchurched pupils was sent to the following other ministers: . . ."

Ministers and their churches take these lists very seriously. Two ministerial committees in the county divide up the names according to addresses close to the homes of the committee members. So anxious are some communities for these lists that they ask for them early in the fall. Most churches seek to recruit these children and their families during the Lenten season; at this time weekday teachers talk to each unchurched pupil personally. Often members of weekday classes offer to stop by and take a classmate along to church on Sunday mornings. (Then follow descriptions of the various methods used by the ministers to follow up their opportunities.)

The staff of the weekday schools cooperates closely and continuously in this recruitment program. Blanks are filled in three times each school year and reported by all teachers to our weekday director, who in turn makes a summarized report to the Committee on Weekday Church Schools. Our weekday schools have an evangelistic outreach, but statistics never tell the whole story. The results must be pictured as they actually happen over the years: a boy becomes an active church youth worker; a father becomes a member of the board of trustees and a Boy Scout sponsor; a mother heads the primary department and enlists the help of her daughter; a family of divided church backgrounds discovers the need for a religious foundation for their home life.

RELATIONS WITH OTHER FAITHS

One might write at length regarding inter-faith cooperation in the weekday church school program. The task of the committee on public relations with respect to relations between the major faiths (as contrasted with relations between the Protestant and other churches operating a community weekday system) is summarized in the following paragraph taken from the *Standards:*[9]

> In practically every community, there should be a board or committee representing all religious faiths. This board should make the plans with public school officials regarding necessary administrative details such as uniform time schedules, preparation and use of common " parent request cards," etc. Through this committee a united religious approach to the public schools and to the community can be made. It can also develop plans for cooperative promotion and publicity.

It is not necessary, and sometimes it is undesirable, to title this committee an " inter-faith committee," as some groups object to the use of the term " faith." The name is of secondary consideration. The important thing is that there be definite understandings and carefully made plans for working together, such as we have described in Chapter III. Communities where these have been overlooked, because of the absence or non-functioning of an interfaith committee, have later found situations develop which it is hard to correct.

A SCHOOL OF THE COMMUNITY

Valuable as a system of weekday church schools is to any community, it is one of many agencies contributing to the character improvement of its boys and girls. While this multiplicity of educational agencies appears at times to bring many complications and a seeming duplication of effort, it is nevertheless an element in a democracy which should not be dispensed with even if it were possible. To

[9] See page 10 of booklet.

do so would be to invite a totalitarian system of education definitely destructive of democracy. Here, as in government itself, " checks and balances " do, and may well continue to function.

As we have noted several times in this volume, the weekday church school has sprung from wholehearted community interest. Its predominant pattern has been that of a community school. It is one of the many expressions of the concern of the total community for the welfare of its children. The weekday church school system should not work alone in smug aloofness from other community agencies. The *Standards* therefore recommend that " to avoid duplication of effort and overlapping, the weekday church school should take into account and join harmoniously with other agencies working with and for children and youth in the community." [10] Here again is a real job for the committee on public relations!

A SCHOOL OF AMERICAN CITIZENSHIP

It is sometimes assumed that only public, tax-supported schools can train for citizenship. Without detracting from the splendid contribution that these schools are making to a loyal and informed citizenship for our democracy, this citizenship training aim, historically speaking, has not been limited to tax-supported schools. As our total American educational program has developed, the citizenship goal has come to play a larger and larger part in all types of school — non-public as well as public. Says a bulletin issued by the United Synagogue Commission on Jewish Education:

Privately financed religious schools in no way contradict the American democratic principles as applied to the

[10] See page 10 of booklet.

education of the young. The public school . . . was primarily established for the purpose of guaranteeing to every child the opportunity to gain sufficient knowledge to enable him to function as a citizen of a democracy. If this objective can be achieved in a privately conducted school, American ideals and practices do not oppose it.[11]

The weekday church school, therefore, takes its place among the non-public schools, which are a recognized part of the American system of education. The place of these non-public schools in our democracy has been indicated in several previous statements in this volume, including the decisions of the United States Supreme Court in the Oregon case (1925), in the McCollum case (1948) and in the Zorach case (1952). The weekday church school, too, is a front-rank agency for citizenship education. The first Co-operative Texts produced for weekday church school use were primarily designed for Christian citizenship training, a purpose which has not lessened as the movement has expanded.

RELATIONSHIPS WITH THE PUBLIC SCHOOL

The relationship of the weekday church school to the public school has been a close one from the earliest years. Its very closeness, encouraged by religious-minded public school leaders as well as church leaders, has been one occasion for its legal difficulties. Now that these have been cleared and the principle of " cooperation with the public school system without using its building or machinery "[12] has been firmly established, it is possible to define the desirable relationships which should be maintained between the two:

[11] *Objectives and Standards for the Congregational School,* pp. 16-17.
[12] Point 3 in "A Ten Point Platform for Weekday Church Schools."

(1) The public school board should recognize the weekday church school as having an important place in the educational life of the children through the week.

(2) The weekday church school system should avoid any organic relationship with the public school system and so conduct its affairs as to be in keeping with the opinion of the United States Supreme Court as rendered in the Champaign Case of March 8, 1948, and the Brooklyn Case of April 28, 1952.

(3) A written agreement regarding the excusal of pupils and other items should be made between the weekday church school board and the local board of education, unless these matters have been cared for by an interfaith committee or board.

(4) Weekday church school workers should cultivate cordial relationships with the public school workers.[13]

---

[13] *Standards for Weekday Church Schools,* pp. 10, 11.

Chapter IX

Winning and Holding Community Support

THE wise Abraham Lincoln once said: " With public sentiment nothing can fail. Without it nothing can succeed. Consequently he who molds public opinion goes deeper than he who enacts statutes or pronounces decisions. He makes statutes and decisions possible to be executed." The truth of this statement is particularly apropos with respect to establishing weekday church schools. There are many who assume that a favorable decision by our highest court almost guarantees a successful program — an assumption which is weak indeed.

For the reaffirmation of the parental right to utilize a portion of the school time for teaching religion we are grateful. For the experiential knowledge which enables us to project the right kind of weekday church school we are likewise appreciative. But these are not enough. The best laid plans will fail without intelligent, widespread, and continued support of the community. It is not only necessary to win this backing by the community in starting a new program, it is just as necessary to hold and increase this support in keeping an established system going.

It is the aim of this chapter to present the factors which make for community interest and demonstrated faith in a weekday church school program and the practical methods of developing them.

As with other committees appointed to develop the program, the recommended committee on publicity and educational promotion has a sizeable job to perform.[1] It is summarized in these paragraphs quoted from the *Standards:*[2]

A strong committee should be chosen to lay the ground work for the interpretation of the weekday church school through the pulpit, press, radio, circulars, letters and periodicals; and by personal visitation in the homes of possible weekday religious education pupils. A clear explanation of the plan providing for the excusal of pupils for religious education should be made to the entire community.

After the program has been inaugurated, the same committee should continue to keep the need for weekday religious education and information regarding the current program before the public with special attention given to parents of pupils and prospective pupils, and to laymen in the cooperating churches.

Promotion and publicity in the churches and cooperating agencies will be of primary importance in the enrollment of pupils in weekday church school classes. The public school system should *not* assist in this enrollment.

The latter portion of this chapter will furnish this important committee with a number of suggestions for fulfilling its responsibilities efficiently.

ENLISTING MANY FRIENDS

We have repeatedly urged the building of a broad base of community support for the weekday program. Just how is this goal to be achieved? A few years ago, when the

[1] See page 79.
[2] See page 11 of booklet.

movement seemed to some to have reached its zenith, attacks upon it and battles over its constitutionality furnished an unexpected stimulus to its development. While not depreciating the fact that in the period of legal confusion the awakened interest and support from many quarters was most welcome, this method of " winning friends and influencing people " is hardly to be counted on as a regular procedure.

In a far western community, it was decided to make use of a mobile classroom as a meeting place for the weekday classes. As the idea gained momentum, the plans for this kind of a classroom expanded in scope and detail. Instead of the usual " trailer " used in a number of places, it was decided to have a driver's cab as a part of the project. Self-contained heating and lighting units were added, as were a three-level floor, a system of mirrors to assist the driver, projectors, a worship center, and other suitable religious education equipment. Starting with the chassis the whole classroom was built by contributions of both money and labor from the entire community. The point to be noted here is the inestimable value of the project for winning the whole citizenry to the weekday church school program. There was scarcely an individual or a group which did not have a stake in the new venture.

Such a worthy project, however, although not in the same category as the legal publicity, is not a sufficiently permanent or inclusive method of winning community support. There is need for a definite, detailed, varied, and continuously operating plan to keep the interest and backing of the largest possible number of persons and groups in the community. How this is done in one community having a strong weekday church school system is shown by the following excerpts from a descriptive article by the director of the system:

The pastor is a key man . . . in the weekday program. When 105 of the 365 Indianapolis pastors are new to the city within the year, it is necessary to " sell " the pastors each year. . . . At a dinner given by a Christian business man, three laymen gave the history of the movement's growth and the financial needs. The Chief Probation Officer . . . told how the program had helped. . . . Three teachers told of their experiences. Following the discussion, every pastor was enthusiastic about the annual observance of Weekday Religious Education Sunday, the second Sunday in October. . . . The entire teaching staff and 48 members of the Board of Directors are available as speakers for that day and through the week that follows.

An Advisory Council enlists the support of church members. . . . The Council meets each year to review the progress of the program. . . . The parents of more than sixty per cent of these (children) claim no church affiliation, and yet all want their children to receive religious training. . . . During the last four years 4,198 children who had not before gone to Sunday school, have enrolled in Sunday school. Other members of their families have been led to the church by the children. . . .

The business men of Indianapolis have been " sold " on the weekday program. This has been done in a number of ways including luncheon meetings for small groups of Christian laymen and the mailing of literature to a selected group. . . . The membership of the Board was increased from 18 to 48 members. Every member makes a contribution to some part of the program through committee work. When they speak the community recognizes their voices as those of leading Christian citizens. . . . Boards of directors of various corporations receive each year a report of the weekday program, and literature is sent individually to each director (including reprints of a two-page story from the *Indianapolis Star Magazine*). . . . A bi-monthly news sheet is issued, telling of the progress of the work and relating human interest stories gleaned by the teachers from their contacts with children from all types of homes.

The weekday program is sponsored by the Committees on Character and Spiritual Education of each local school's Parent-Teacher Association. The committee members visit in the homes to secure the parents' signatures for the release of their children for an hour's study each week.

The annual graduation service is one of the major program events of the year and focuses public attention on the weekday program. . . .

The Board's Promotion Committee is composed of two pastors, two members of the Indianapolis Council of Church Women, editors of two daily papers, presidents of two publicity firms, two public relations men, and two radio program directors. This committee outlines the year's program and is now projecting a five-year "selling" program. . . .

The most important part of " selling the community " is that the persons involved in the program are themselves " sold " on the program. In addition to the Board members there are thousands of people in Indianapolis who believe thoroughly in the program of weekday religious education. Indeed, 1,408 people are working on committees of one kind or another. Each year the Administrative Director sends a New Year's letter to these volunteer workers who have helped to make the program possible for the girls and boys.[3]

RESOLVING MISUNDERSTANDINGS

It sometimes happens that support of a weekday church school program is withheld by certain individuals or groups in the community or that occasionally a determined and

[3] Pfleiderer, F. A., " Selling Weekday Religious Education," *International Journal of Religious Education.*

violent opposition is voiced. It is not our intention to discuss or refute the arguments made by these groups, but to suggest what should be done in such situations.

In the pamphlet, *Remember the Weekday to Teach Religion Thereon*,[4] this question is found: " Should the plan be put in operation by only a small part of the church groups?" The answer given is: " If some of the groups have not had opportunity to consider the plan, other groups should not proceed hastily. The plan succeeds to the extent that the whole community is well informed and sympathetic. On the other hand, after a reasonable time for consideration, it is not fair for those not desiring to use the plan to oppose others wishing to do so." This suggests two procedures: first, thorough and careful study of the kind we have already indicated; and second, the right and necessity of those who want the program to proceed after a reasonable period of consideration by the community.

The possible misunderstandings may be in the area of legality, of educational desirability, or of practical administration. Whatever the area of questioning, help is available for those who may wish to have disputed issues clarified. A request should be sent to denominational or interdenominational educational agencies, area or national, for informative literature and if necessary the services of persons with knowledge and experience with the problems. Note the phrase, "if necessary." It is often better not to bring in outsiders, unless and until local resources have been exhausted.

Fortunately the legal questions have been largely settled as we stated in Chapter II. But other questions still remain and will remain as the movement continues to expand.

[4] National Council of Churches, p. 13.

Such questions should be considered challenges to continuous improvement rather than handicaps.

The wise strategy, in forestalling or dealing with differences, is to follow a positive and constructive " live and let live " policy. One community[5] found itself divided with respect to which way was best for the several religious groups to teach religion on the weekday. Two groups preferred the parochial school. One group thought its after-school program most suitable. Another group involving a large number of churches was in favor of the weekday church school plan of the type we are describing. Wise leadership in this community led to the formation of a community (inter-faith) committee[6] in which the leaders of all groups meet for friendly consultation and fellowship. In this community-wide common interest in religious education for the largest possible number of children there has developed a common and sympathetic understanding in spite of method differences. None of the groups takes an opposition attitude to the preferred programs of the others.

EDUCATIONAL PROMOTION

Publicity alone is not sufficient for winning and holding community support for the weekday program, as we have indicated in a previous section. Note that the name of the committee charged with this responsibility is the " Committee on Publicity and Educational Promotion." Whatever is done should be educational in aim and in method. In a committee report of the Weekday Religious Education Section[7] we find some helpful principles of interpretation, such as:

[5] Evansville, Indiana.
[6] See also pp. 34 and 115.
[7] A unit of the National Council of Churches. This report is out of print.

Interpretation should be *inclusive*. It should deal with large aspects, major activities and interests, including all phases of the program.

Interpretation should be *continuous*. Only spectacular, high pressure campaigns once a year or sporadic interpretation is not good publicity.

Interpretation should be *understandable*. It should be rich in concrete nouns, live verbs, with relatively few adjectives, direct quotations, short direct statements. Do not use professional jargon. Such words as " areas of experience," " motivation for learning," etc., are not the layman's language.

Interpretation should be *honest*. Publicity in the commercial world is based on the assumption that action comes when emotions have been aroused. Understanding is not sufficient. There must be color. Visualizing and dramatizing the values and methods of the schools will give color, but must be kept true to the situation and honestly depict the actual happenings. Telling half-truths or using only the spectacular high pressure method is not good publicity. Public confidence once lost is difficult to regain.

Interpretation and publicity must be *dignified* but *aggressive*. The weekday church schools must be respected as well as understood.

THEY DO IT THESE WAYS

We have seen the necessity, both for winning initial support and for holding that support, of at least a year's thorough study and a resultant fool-proof plan of school organization. We have pointed out the job of the publicizing committee and the need for enlisting many friends, exemplified by the story of how one successful weekday system has won them. We have suggested how misunderstandings may be resolved and the principles for a program of publicity which is truly interpretive and educational.

We shall conclude the chapter by reporting a variety of promotional methods which have been used by weekday systems. These are selected in part from a survey made by a committee of the Weekday Religious Education Section.[8] Local publicity committees may well use these various demonstrated methods as a check list in planning their publicity strategy. The order of listing does not indicate their relative value which will vary with communities and circumstances.

PERSON-TO-PERSON CONTACTS

Home visitation has great interpretive value. In the stronger systems a portion of each teacher's time is set apart for contacting parents. Some systems enlist the services of other helpers — " room mothers," retired parish visitors, special visiting committees, and pastors. A first purpose is to secure enrollment in the weekday classes. But equally important is explanation of the program and the part the parents have in it. A very significant opportunity, in visiting parents, is to discover the needs of the children and give special help to each one, particularly to problem children and often problem parents. Financial solicitation is rarely a purpose of these home contacts, and wisely so, except as a distinctly separate project.

The children themselves are probably the best promoters of the weekday church school. Their own interest in the teaching leads them to tell others about it — their parents, other adults, and their child friends. These latter they invite to the weekday classes and also to their Sunday church schools, if they are not already attending. Older children sometimes speak about the weekday program at church

[8] " Interpreting and Publicizing the Weekday Church School," McWhirter, Mary Esther, editor. (Out of print.)

meetings. Using the children in special programs has strong selling appeal for the program — at graduation services, in choirs and dramas, on radio and television programs.

Nothing can take the place of face-to-face conferences between the leaders of the weekday program and other community leaders — the ministers; P.-T.A. officers; leaders of character-building agencies; public school officials; business, professional, and labor leaders; and other key persons. Wise is the publicity committee which systematically plans to interview these community leaders one by one.

While the direction and teaching service in a weekday system are the responsibilities of professionally trained persons, there is a large place for lay participation in the program. Laymen have a large part in the board and committee activities in making policies and in the kind of specialized service which we have described in this volume, that is, working on the curriculum, finance, public relations, and publicity committees. They also assist the program by escorting pupils and acting as secretaries, hostesses, musical leaders, and project directors. Through these experiences they become better fitted to work in the Sunday and vacation church schools of their churches and, under some conditions, to take teaching responsibilities in the weekday church school itself. The larger the number of lay partners working in the weekday system, the stronger becomes the community support.

GROUP CONTACTS

There are many opportunities for publicizing the program to groups of persons. One of the most important of such groups is the children of the Sunday church school. In a great variety of ways the privilege of enrolling in the weekday church school is presented to them — in personal visits of pastors in the church homes, through the church calendar and mail contacts, through the teachers of the Sunday classes, through sermons, and through speakers representing the weekday system. The core membership of weekday classes is represented in the children of the churches. The winning of un-churched children is conditioned in large part upon the interest of the church and the children it has already reached.

Another opportunity for educational promotion is found in various adult groups. Such groups reported in the survey included women's clubs, ministers' associations, councils of church women, civic organizations and service clubs, church congregations and adult classes and organizations, denominational area meetings and meetings of the council of churches in the community, and college and theological seminary classes.

One of the most fruitful group contacts is secured through visitation of the classes. To see a good weekday church school class in session is to be sold on the program. Consequently, those who wish to interpret the program plan to have members of various groups pay a visit to the school. Among them are pastors, parents, selected groups of church workers and public school teachers and officers, students in training for religious leadership, delegations from communities considering a program, officers and committee members of the local weekday system, and various lay groups such as we have mentioned above. It goes without saying that careful planning is required for such visitation. Said one weekday church school director: " We have never had a visitor who did not go away with a better understanding of what we were doing."

Since the weekday church school is basically a school created by parents, it is highly important to contact parents in groups as well as individually. To do this some weekday systems develop a plan for meetings of parents for this special purpose. While it is generally considered unwise to create a special parents' association for the weekday program, some systems plan for a meeting of their parents once a year. The more common practice is to reach the parents as a group through the parent-teacher associations of the community. Experience has shown that such contacts are the more fruitful if the children from the weekday classes occasionally have a special part in the program, preferably one of the very early programs of the school year.

The opportunities for interpretation through the local lay leadership training schools are excellent. The weekday teachers often teach in these schools. The weekday classes are utilized as observation and laboratory centers for the leadership school. Courses on weekday religious education are given and frequently some person representing the system is asked to address the school. In weekday systems whose teachers have had insufficient training there is usually a requirement that they increase their efficiency by taking these leadership courses.

There are often other special group meetings at which the weekday program may be publicized — community coordinating councils, fairs, union religious services, teas, and other events.

USING PRINTED MATERIALS

One of the most commonly used means of educational promotion is the distribution of printed materials of which there is a great variety — leaflets prepared locally, literature from denominational and interdenominational offices, posters, copies of special issues of religious education journals, articles in local council and church bulletins. Human interest story sheets, samples of pupils' original work, cartoons and line drawings suggest the wide variety of locally developed materials which may be utilized. The Department of Weekday Religious Education of the National Council of Churches has issued a number of pamphlets which have been widely used in local communities.

Some weekday systems have built up a library of books and other printed materials which are loaned to individuals and groups desiring to become acquainted with the program or various aspects of it. Reviews of these documents and current articles are presented at various meetings.

Letters, usually mimeographed, are used extensively in informing interested persons regarding the local program. Parents are sent a number of letters throughout the year — letters asking for pupil enrollment, letters explaining the course of study and making suggestions for home cooperation, invitations to attend special events at the weekday school, letters following absences (personal and handwritten), notes reporting the progress of the students. Communications are also sent to pastors and members of the various other interested groups we have enumerated, giving information and asking for co-operation in the program. The children, also, often write letters to their parents and other persons regarding the school activities.

Newspaper publicity is indispensable to the success of a local weekday program. For the most part weekday church schools have received excellent backing from the press in the form of news articles, editorials, announcements, and special featuring including pictures. The opening of the school year and graduation exercises are strategic times to secure newspaper publicity. Special projects also furnish occasions for it. Persons related to the press may well be on the committee on publicity and educational promotion. In any case the committee or persons in charge of this publicity should obviously prepare the material in the best possible form and conform to the editorial requirements of the papers.

VISUAL AND AUDIO AIDS

A great variety of visualization methods are used by weekday church school systems to publicize their work. Posters and placards are a common means, and are often made by the pupils themselves, which gives added value to their use. They are displayed in churches, commercial establishments, and at various meetings in the community. Maps of the community showing the location of the weekday schools and the areas not yet served by the program are an effective promotional aid. Photographs and snapshots may be utilized in many ways. They may show classrooms, class activities, worship centers, projects undertaken — in fact everything which is a part of the program. These have historical as well as current value and may be classified in scrapbooks for showing to present and prospective supporters of the program. Stereopticon slides made from these photographs are equally helpful. Charts and graphs are other means. They are used in reports, bulletins, posters, and other publicity channels.

A number of weekday systems have had movies made of their classes and activities and show them at various meetings. Often other communities not yet organized for weekday work borrow them to interpret the plan. Filmstrips are being used more and more for publicity purposes.

The use of exhibits is a practice followed by most weekday systems. They are placed in churches, at parent-teacher meetings, in store windows, at all kinds of religious and community gatherings. They include many features — courses of study, Bibles and hymnbooks, worship centers, promotional literature, samples of pupils' work, in fact whatever will help to inform the friends and general public.

The use of the radio for publicity purposes is now a common practice. When the programs are well prepared the stations are glad to give time for this interesting community activity. Various kinds of presentations are made — typical class sessions, interviews and discussions, skits and plays, stories, and spot announcements.

Television also is being utilized to interpret the weekday program. Groups of children from weekday classes portray class sessions, worship activities, and other class projects which are very effective in showing the kind of training which goes on in the weekday church school.

USING THE PUBLIC SCHOOL SYSTEM

In the past some weekday church schools made use of the public school system to publicize their programs. In the light of the United States Supreme Court decisions in both the McCollum and Zorach cases the use of any form of public school machinery as well as buildings is considered unconstitutional. Therefore *no method of promotion may be used in the public school.* This does not mean, however, that public school leaders may not give it their personal unofficial support. They are free to assist at many points in promoting the program as citizens interested in the welfare of the community, and to take a co-operative attitude toward it.

Chapter X

Charting the Future

WEEKDAY religious education will be either a huge success or a grand ' flop ' ! " In these colloquial words an outstanding religious educator of the past generation [1] once expressed his opinion as to the future of the program we have been describing. Were he speaking today, he might make the same prediction, although with much less emphasis upon the likelihood of failure. Things have been happening in the movement — most of which may be counted on the success side of the balance sheet.

CAREFUL GUIDANCE

This able religious educator whom we have quoted was a member of the Findings Committee appointed by the Religious Education Association at its convention in 1922. This committee, as we stated in Chapter II, pointed out the potentialities of the new type of school, but also warned of possible mistakes in its development. As the movement continued to expand, with more caution on the part of its advocates as a result of this appraisal, the International Council of Religious Education took note of it and in 1941 adopted the following statement of policy:

[1] Herbert W. Gates, General Secretary, Division of Christian Education, Congregational and Christian Churches.

In view of the great interest in weekday religious education in many forms, the present confusion as to best procedure, and the urgent request for help from the field, the International Council of Religious Education states its policy concerning weekday religious education as follows:

" With regard to the Weekday Church School in cooperation with the public school on released or dismissed time, the Council is convinced of the contributions which the weekday church school, when conducted according to the standards set in Educational Bulletin #601, ' The Weekday Church School,' makes to the total program of Christian education, and recommends that its Committee and Director continue to pursue the policy of wise direction and careful guidance of weekday church schools in accordance with the standards for this work adopted by the Council."

In 1949, following the decision of the United States Supreme Court in the McCollum case, the International Council issued a more detailed policy statement to insure conformity to the legal requirements for these schools of religion and to reaffirm the Council's wholehearted belief in the weekday program.[2] When the National Council of Churches was formed in 1950, its Division of Christian Education accepted these two policy statements with approval and the National Council's General Board twice voted legal support of the program when the Zorach case was before the courts. Throughout the period of legal fighting for existence the Department of Weekday Religious Education continued to give guidance both with respect to possible legal infringements and particularly to the maintenance of high educational standards for the program.

[2] " Statement of Policy Regarding Weekday Religious Education," Division of Christian Education, National Council of Churches. Excerpts from the longer statement are quoted in the pamphlet, *Remember the Weekday to Teach Religion Thereon.*

This accent on quality found expression in "A Ten Point Platform for Weekday Church Schools," which has highlighted the counsel given to local weekday systems since the establishment of the Department of Weekday Religious Education in 1942:

1. A year of planning before launching the program.
2. All religious groups working closely together.
3. Parents accepting their responsibility for the school and supporting it in every way.
4. Cooperation with the public school system without using its buildings or machinery.
5. A representative and reliable weekday church school board continuously on the job.
6. A course of education in religion as well planned and implemented to its purposes as the courses in the public schools are to theirs.
7. Teachers as well trained for teaching religion as the public school teachers are for their work.
8. A supervisor — trained, experienced, and religious — working with every school.
9. An expenditure per pupil (in proportion to the teaching time) equal to that for his public school education.
10. The spirit as well as the letter of the law preserved in all relationships.[3]

This platform was followed in 1950 by the adoption of the detailed set of *Standards for Weekday Church Schools* to which reference has been made repeatedly throughout this volume. The committee which prepared them was composed of workers with extensive local and national experience with weekday church schools. They were concerned with the future of the program as well as its more

[3] *Remember the Weekday to Teach Religion Thereon* (National Council of Churches), p. 16.

immediate needs, following the lead of the thoughtful pioneers whose prophesies and counsels we have quoted. The same concern has been expressed by an outstanding Christian education leader, Richard Hoiland:

> Weekday religious education in America will survive only as the need for the highest possible standard of work is not only recognized but accepted and taken into account. In other words, no other factor will be so determinative of the future of the weekday movement as its own inner strength and quality.[4]

MAKING GOOD

It is the general conviction of religious educators that the weekday church school is making good. Let us note a few of its accomplishments. In those communities where the recommended standards have been followed, it is a most effective school of religion. In one such community a local director of Christian education raised this question: " The children of my Sunday church school are also attending the community weekday church school. At the latter they have learned as much about the Bible as one could hope for. What shall we teach them on Sunday?" A strong emphasis in weekday church schools has been the endeavor to apply religious teachings to life situations. This is exemplified by a boy's prayer made in all sincerity and reverence (in a session following a rain, when the more foresighted girls shared their rain togs with the boys and enabled the entire class to reach the church without getting wet): " Dear God, we thank Thee for girls and galoshes!"

The weekday church school has proven to be a most effective evangelistic and missionary agency. On the aver-

---

[4] " The Future Depends on Quality," *International Journal of Religious Education*.

age, in the co-operative type of weekday system, one fourth of the children enrolled have had no church or church school connection. In our large industrial type communities the percentage is much higher, often fifty or sixty per cent of the weekday enrollment being classified as having no church connections. In most of these cases this means that their families, too, are unrelated to a church.

This school has also brought about a closer relationship between the three agencies most responsible for the child's education — the home, the public school, and the church. Separately they are our most important educational agencies; when they work in co-operation, their efficiency quotient is multiplied.

This weekday school of religion has likewise demonstrated, in a manner unsurpassed, that the churches can work together. The vast majority of the Protestant weekday church school systems are of the co-operative type. It would seem that a miracle indeed has been performed when our churches commit the teaching of their children to a school in which curriculum, teachers, and classroom facilities are selected without regard to denominational lines. In addition to this co-operation within the Protestant group, there is demonstrated an unusual degree of inter-faith co-operation. Many stories might be told to illustrate this growing understanding and friendliness across faith lines, both on the part of adult leaders in the program and the children. The result has been, not an emphasis upon supposed divisiveness, but upon respect and appreciation both for differences and common goals.

Another question asked about the weekday church school program is whether it makes for improved conduct. Scientifically accurate measurements of the behavior of children taking weekday church school courses are as difficult to secure as they are in the case of other character-building agencies — the public and private schools, the youth agencies, and even the churches. But there are strong convictions that each of these makes for a better community and for a higher type of personal and social conduct. Such a conviction with respect to the efficacy of the weekday church school is voiced in a personal letter by Joe H. Glasser, Judge of Garfield County, Enid, Oklahoma:

> Juvenile delinquency in the County . . . was becoming progressively worse each year until a noticeable correction in the pattern was observed among a group level of youngsters who were members of the first class to participate in the Associated Church program for released time teaching. Therefore, the only reasonable conclusion to be derived from such an analysis was that Christian education, without doctrinal teaching, had caused the noticeable decline in unlawful behavior characteristics of those youngsters who participated in the program when compared with the activities of the older children who did not so participate.
>
> I am firmly convinced that releasing children from academic instruction in the public schools for one hour each week to enable the students to receive Christian education, which the majority of the students would not otherwise receive, is the greatest step the community has taken in answer to the problem of juvenile delinquency.

It is no wonder that this new school of religion has spread from shore to shore in America. It has had its ups and downs, but the general trend has been definitely upward. It is estimated that the churches in three thousand communities, large and small, in almost every state are using this plan to teach religion to approximately three million children of all faiths.

Aside from these direct contributions to the religious education of American children and youth, the weekday church school movement has made significant concomitant contributions. It has kept alive, against no little opposition, the importance of religion in all education. It has spurred and encouraged educational leaders to place a larger emphasis upon religion in the public schools. It has been a strong factor in retarding the growth of Protestant parochial schools. Unintentionally, it has caused America to face the need for a more accurate interpretation of the First Amendment, defining the points at which church and state shall be separate and those at which they may cooperate for the common good. It has presented to the religious world an example of Christian education leadership second to no other in quality of training, consecration to service, and unusual self-sacrifice. For both these direct and related services to religion and democracy we should be grateful indeed.

OVERCOMING LIMITATIONS

It is true of weekday church schools, as of all types of schools, that they must work under certain handicaps more or less inherent in their organizational patterns. These limitations are not to be looked upon as final but as challenges to improvement. One of these is the short time allotted for this teaching program — commonly one hour each week. It is to be hoped and expected that the "complementary school" plan, discussed later in this chapter, will be a means of overcoming this time difficulty. In any case, it should be pointed out that, if we are to dismiss as useless a one hour teaching opportunity, many other one hour programs would have to be discarded — Sunday church school classes and evening fellowship meetings, the one-hour-a-week class in any school subject.

This time limitation has also caused some weekday as well as other teachers of religion to confine their teaching to imparting information. This need not be. Those teachers who have imagination and faith in the value of creative experiences will find fruitful methods of using and supplementing the short period in such ways as we described in the section, " A Rich Weekday Curriculum," in Chapter IV.

The best teaching, particularly in the areas of religion and character development, must include individual guidance of the pupil. When the teaching load of a weekday teacher runs up into hundreds of pupils taught each week, personal attention to even a few of them seems impossible. But it need not be so, as some weekday systems have demonstrated. When the kind of program we have recommended is established, a considerable part of the teachers' time can be given to helping individual pupils. Whether or not this at-first-sight limitation is overcome depends largely on the willingness of the system's planners to provide for this central element in good religious education by setting aside time for it in the schedule of the teachers.

NO PUBLIC SCHOOL ASSISTANCE

At its beginning there was a belief on the part of some of its friends that a program of weekday religious education needed and should have the substantial aid of the public school. There were various ways in which this assistance manifested itself. The writer and other critical students of the movement warned against this point of view. Gradually it has tended to disappear, until today the vast majority of systems have disavowed various forms of aid on the part of the public school. Unfortunately, it required court action to focus attention on these practices. From now on weekday religious education on released time must be considered a church and not a public school program.

IMPORTANT ORGANIZATIONAL ISSUES

In projecting the future of the weekday church school we would like to point out what seem to be significant issues which the movement must meet and solve. Upon the answers given to these either-or alternatives, largely organizational in nature, depends the kind and quality of weekday church schools for tomorrow's generation of children.

One of these issues is that of conducting the school on released or dismissed time. The differences between these patterns has been pointed out, and the weaknesses of the latter indicated. We believe that few communities will be willing to adopt such a substitute for a program which includes religion within the school day and the formal education program.

A second issue is that of the time schedule of excusal adopted. If educationally efficient weekday church school systems are to be the rule, this can be brought about only by means of a staggered or distributed schedule of excusal. This allows for full-time, trained teachers, a basic consideration when religion is to be treated as a subject deserving as much attention as secular studies.

Another issue is whether the dominant pattern for weekday church schools is to be denominational or interdenominational. While some religious groups prefer and have the right to conduct a denominational program during the time of pupil excusal, the widespread adoption of this pattern would both multiply the problems of local organization and administration and result in the loss of the gains we have enumerated as inherent in the co-operative pattern.

A fourth issue is whether Protestantism is ready to assume the cost of this kind of religious education. It has long been habituated to meager support of its Christian education agencies. To pay the hour-for-hour cost of teaching religion as effectively as arithmetic is taught, is a new idea. Many communities have demonstrated that they have gladly accepted this step-up in raising their budgets for Christian education. If others will follow their lead, the successful meeting of this issue is assured.

PROTESTANTISM'S FORMAL SCHOOL CHOICES

In extending its total program so as to give larger attention to religious education within legal and customary school hours, there are three choices open to Protestantism.

The first of these choices is to establish parochial schools. In fact, there is a growing interest in such a policy on the part of some Protestant groups, both those which have traditionally maintained such schools and others which now believe that this is the best answer to the present situation. The general attitude among Protestants, however, is reflected in a policy document of the Division of Christian Education of the National Council of Churches: "Should our Protestant churches consider seriously the building of church-related elementary and secondary schools on an increasing scale? We believe our present answer should be 'No.' We defend the right of all religious groups to carry on church-related education at any level, elementary, secondary, or higher, and the right of parents to send their children to these schools if they so desire. But while we defend the right we do not believe it should be exercised at the elementary and secondary levels." [5]

A second choice for Protestants is that of depending upon the public school to carry a considerable portion of the responsibility for religious education. (1) Some of them would have the public school include in its program all the religious activities that will get by in a local community. (2) Others believe that teaching spiritual values in the public school is the answer. In this group there are two schools of thought — one holding that " the term ' spiritual values ' . . . carries no explicit or necessary reference to religious or divine authority or sanction";[6] the other holding that a belief in God and the use of religious resources are essential to any effective spiritual values program. (3) Still others assert that, in dealing with religion in the public school, the emphasis should be limited to a factual study of religion, or teaching *about* religion.

The first proposal is questionable both ethically and legally. What can be achieved through a spiritual values program depends, so far as religion is concerned, upon the extent to which the program is motivated by an avowed faith in God and the resources of religion are utilized. As to teaching *about* religion, we quote with approval the comment of an outstanding religious educator:

" Any such plan for religion in public education will not take the place of what churches and synagogues have been

[5] *Report of the Committee on Religion and Public Education* (National Council of Churches), p. 5.

[6] Brubacher, John S., ed., *The Public Schools and Spiritual Values,* Seventh Yearbook of the John Dewey Society (Harpers), p. 8.

doing in religious education. About all that can be expected is that this will create a favorable climate for religious education and provide foundations on which more specifically Christian teaching may be based." [7]

THE COMPLEMENTARY SCHOOL PLAN

A third choice for our Protestant churches now appears to be in the making — an expanded weekday church school with classes meeting during school hours and with a religious education curriculum adapted to the needs of each local community. For such a complementary type of school (complementary, in that it does what cannot be done by the public school) we have two tested and currently operating precedents, aside from the weekday church school program we have been describing in this volume. One of these precedents is the " seminary " program begun in 1912 by the Church of Jesus Christ of Latter Day Saints and now established in more than one hundred communities. The other precedent is the growing practice in many communities throughout America of having children, whose primary enrollment is in a parochial school, take some of their courses in the public school, even to the extent in one reported instance of a " fifty-fifty " program.

The acceptance and implementation of the complementary school plan envisions the development of a community educational campus located at the center of each child-population area. The central and major educational unit would be the public school, in which it would be expected all children would be enrolled for most of their work. Clustered about it would be the units erected by the

[7] Vieth, Paul H., *Religious Education,* Vol. XLVIII, p. 79.

churches, preferably on a co-operative basis, in which a religious education program would be conducted. In addition there would be units established by the other character-building agencies working with children. The exact proportion of courses and other activities carried on in these several units would vary with local community situations and needs. Under such a plan and with such a campus, a new pattern of co-operation in the total education of children and youth would develop, which in most instances would make unnecessary the present type of private and parochial schools which occupy the total school time of the pupil.

In addition to the obvious religious education opportunities afforded by such a complementary school program, there are certain other values which would accrue if such a program were to become general.

It represents a middle-of-the-road approach to the parochial-public school problem and might persuade those, who now see no alternative to maintaining parochial schools, to voluntarily give them up entirely or greatly reduce their numbers. It would enable Protestants generally to continue and increase their moral support of the public schools without reservations. Such a plan would also free the public schools from the difficulties inherent in the present pressure for more religion in the schools. It would relieve the fears of those who see, in the tendency of the public schools to take over more and more of the waking time of the child, a strong drift toward totalitarianism. It would require and encourage Protestant churches to take religious education more seriously. Further, it would be a strong factor in lifting the educational standards of the various other teaching programs now sponsored by the churches.

Weekday religious education as we have presented it in this volume — a system of part-time church schools meeting during school hours and complementary to our public school program — offers our Protestant churches a great opportunity. It also confronts them with a series of challenges which test their historic evangelistic and teaching ministries. We state some of these challenges:

1. The weekday church school presents an opportunity for Protestantism to prove that it believes in a teaching church.

2. Through weekday church schools Protestantism may demonstrate the truth that a child's education is sadly neglected if it ignores his spiritual quotient.

3. In the weekday church school there is an opportunity to show that religion can be taught just as earnestly and as skillfully as teaching is done to meet any other need of child life.

4. The establishment and continuance of church schools built on this pattern will prove also that religious education can and should take place on the weekday as well as on Sunday.

5. In the development of weekday church schools an opportunity has been afforded for Protestantism to show that it can raise up a consecrated teaching order.

6. The continued growth of weekday church schools meeting high educational standards is also a test of Protestantism's scale of values. It has generously backed our splendid public school system. Will it pay as much for the teaching of religion as for secular subjects?

7. In the pattern first set for weekday church schools

and now accepted as the official policy of co-operative American Protestantism there is opportunity for it to re-affirm its belief in the separation of church and state as expressed in the First Amendment.

8. Weekday church schools open the door to inter-church co-operation. Protestantism is challenged to continue and extend this co-operative program.

The members of the Denominational Executives Section of the Division of Christian Education of the National Council of Churches, representing many Protestant bodies, have been impressed with these opportunities and, in an individually signed statement, have declared their faith in the weekday church school on released time, as follows:

WE BELIEVE IN THE WEEKDAY CHURCH SCHOOL

The church has for many years recognized the need for supplementing the Sunday church school with other periods of instruction during the week. Classes have been held on Saturday and after regular school hours. During the past half century there has also been marked development in a program that uses an hour or more a week of " regular school time " for religious instruction outside the public school building. This has come to be known as " the weekday church school on released time."

After a period of uncertainty, the legal questions relative to the program of the released time church school have now been cleared by the United States Supreme Court. At the same time, the growing recognition in our churches of the importance of Christian education and the increasing concern in the nation as a whole for the moral and spiritual welfare of all our children, have combined to create a greater interest in the possibilities of the weekday church school with special attention being focused on the released time program.

We support and encourage every effort to strengthen the total weekday church school program. At this time we take the opportunity to reaffirm our faith particularly in the *released time* weekday church school as an effective instrument for Christian teaching and we assume our share of responsibility for its future direction.

WE BELIEVE in the weekday church school on released time because —

It includes the teaching of religion within the framework of the child's formal education

It emphasizes the place which religion should have in the weekday life of our boys and girls as well as on Sunday

It greatly expands our churches' total program of Christian education

It enrolls large numbers of boys and girls hitherto unreached by Christian teaching

It acquaints its pupils with the lessons of the Bible and with the life and work of our Lord and Savior, Jesus Christ

It is an expression of the deepest needs and the most earnest purposes of American citizens

It has proved its effectiveness by many years of successful experience

WE BELIEVE FURTHER —

That our churches should now give their positive approval to this Christian teaching agency and include weekday church schools within their total programs of Christian education, making them schools *of* the church, *by* the church, and *for* the church

That weekday church schools are neither substitutes for, nor in competition with other church-sponsored agencies of Christian education or whatever religious emphases may be legally included in the programs of our public schools

[150]

That, in the weekday church school, especially on released
time, we have found a practical way to include the
teaching of religion in the total education of American children and at the same time to give deserved and
wholehearted support to our public schools

That our churches should raise their present level of financial support for Christian education to make possible
the quality of teaching represented in the best weekday church school programs

WE THEREFORE CALL UPON OUR CHURCHES,
individually and in co-operation —

To give thorough study to weekday religious education on
released time, that they may be well informed as to
its educational requirements, its costs, and its values

To explore the possibilities of establishing such programs
in the communities in which they are located

To initiate limited experimental centers for the purpose of
demonstrating how a high-grade weekday church
school program should operate

To develop — on the basis of such study, exploration,
and experimentation — community-wide programs of
weekday religious education on released time for all
the communities served by our churches

IN WITNESS of our faith in the weekday church
school, we have hereby subscribed our names, individually
and as members of the National Denominational Executives' Section of the Division of Christian Education of the
National Council of the Churches of Christ in the United
States of America.

For Further Study

The following list of materials for further study is necessarily limited. For example, no attempt is made to include the many articles on the subject to be found in religious and educational journals. It is suggested that the reader send for the latest revision of a mimeographed " Bibliography for Weekday Religious Education " which contains magazine as well as other references to study materials.

OLDER BOOKS

Persons making an extensive historical study may wish to consult certain earlier books. These are now out of print, but may be available in libraries. Among them are:

Cope, H. F., *The Weekday Church School* (George H. Doran Company, 1921).

Forsyth, N. F., *Weekday Church Schools, Their Organization and Administration* (Methodist Book Concern, 1930).

Gift, F. U., *Weekday Religious Education* (United Lutheran Publishing House, 1926).

Gove, F. S., *Religious Education on Public School Time* (Harvard University, 1926).

Hauser, C. A., *Latent Religious Resources in Public Education* (Heidelberg Press, 1924).

Jackson, J. K., and Malmberg, C. F., *Religious Education and the State* (Doubleday Doran, 1928).

Squires, W. A., *The Weekday Church School* (The Presbyterian Board of Publication and Sunday School Work, 1924).

Young, T. S., *Weekday Church School Methods* (Judson Press, 1924).

EARLIER SURVEYS

In the earlier periods of the development of weekday church schools, several comprehensive surveys were made. The facts and findings of these are of considerable value today. These are now out of print, but may be available in libraries. Among them are:

A survey conducted by Erwin L. Shaver for the Religious Education Association in 1921–22 securing data from 324 schools.

Published in *Religious Education* for April, 1922, and reprinted in the book, *Weekday Religious Education* (Doran. H. F. Cope, ed.).

A survey made by P. Henry Lotz in 1923 covering 109 schools. Published under the title, *Current Weekday Religious Education* (Abingdon Press).

A study entitled " Measurable Moral and Religious Outcomes of Weekday Religious Instruction " made by Edward R. Bartlett and submitted to the Graduate School of Northwestern University in 1933 and reprinted under this title by *Religious Education* in January, 1934, issue. Abstract of dissertation available in *Summaries of Ph.D. Dissertations,* Volume I, 1933.

A survey of 383 communities made by Donald R. Gorham in 1934 and published under the title, *The Status of Protestant Weekday Church Schools in the United States.* The School of Religious Education of the Eastern Baptist Theological Seminary, Philadelphia, Pennsylvania.

Books in Current Use

Only one book of recent date deals specifically and exclusively with weekday religious education on released time. This is *Teaching the Multitudes* by Minor C. Miller (Beacon Publishers, Bridgewater, Virginia, 1944). It discusses the movement from the standpoint both of theory and practice — organization, finance, teachers, curriculum, and standards.

Orientation in Religious Education (Abingdon Press, Nashville, Tennessee, 1950. P. Henry Lotz, ed.) contains a chapter (Number 22) on " The Weekday Church School," describing problems faced by the movement as well as a brief history of it.

In *The New Education and Religion* (Association Press, New York, 1945) J. Paul Williams discusses the pros and cons of weekday church schools as one of the possible solutions of the problems of relating public education and religion.

Recent Surveys

In addition to a number of unpublished theses and dissertations made by graduate students, two significant published studies may be mentioned:

"The Status of Religious Education in the Public Schools," published by the National Education Association, June, 1949, based on a study concluded in May, 1949. Single copies are available from the N.E.A. at 1201 Sixteenth Street, N.W., Washington, D. C., for 25 cents. It should be read carefully in conjunction with a "Memorandum" regarding it which is available without charge from the Department of Weekday Religious Education of the National Council of Churches.

A study by Lois V. McClure, *Weekday Religious Education at the High School Level,* submitted to the Graduate School of Northwestern University in partial fulfillment of the degree of Master of Arts, 1951. This study was sponsored jointly by the Departments of Research and Weekday Religious Education of the National Council of Churches. Reprint copies of a condensation which appeared in *Religious Education* may be secured from the National Council of Churches at 60 cents each.

Decisions of the United States Supreme Court

The governing and other opinions of the Court in the case of McCollum versus Board of Education, Champaign County, Illinois, delivered March 8, 1948.

The governing and other opinions of the Court in the case of Zorach versus Clauson et al, delivered April 28, 1952.

Pamphlets and Bulletins

Among the various practical helps, available to those interested in establishing a weekday church school program or strengthening one now in operation, are those listed below. Send to the Department of Weekday Religious Education for any of the following and for the latest list of "Literature Available."

Statement of Policy Regarding Weekday Religious Education
Remember the Weekday To Teach Religion Thereon — Brief answers to questions commonly asked about Weekday Church Schools
Standards for Weekday Church Schools
Weekday Church School Texts (*The Co-operative Series*)